The Essence
of Strategic
Decision Making

The Essence of Strategic Decision Making

Charles R. Schwenk
Indiana University

Lexington Books *1988*

D.C. Heath and Company/Lexington, Massachusetts/Toronto

Library of Congress Cataloging-in-Publication Data

Schwenk, Charles R.
The essence of strategic decision making.

Bibliography: p.
Includes index.
1. Decision-making.   2. Corporate management.
3. Decision-making—Case studies.   4. Corporate
management—Case studies.   I. Title.
HD30.23.S39   1988   658.4'03   86-80040
ISBN 0-669-13023-0 (alk. paper)

Published simultaneously in Canada
Printed in the United States of America
International Standard Book Number: 0-669-13023-0
Library of Congress Catalog Card Number: 86-80040

The paper used in this publication meets the minimum requirements of
American National Standard for Information Sciences—Permanence
of Paper for Printed Library Materials, ANSI Z39.48-1984.

88 89 90 91 92 8 7 6 5 4 3 2 1

Contents

Tables and Figures

Tables

Figures

Preface

This book deals with the use of multiple perspectives in explaining strategic decisions. It focuses on three basic perspectives that may be used by those who attempt to understand their own organizations' decisions. These were first described by Graham Allison (1971). Allison's typology provides the framework for this book, in which I review the strategic management literature dealing with decision processes and factors that affect decision outcomes.

There are many typologies dealing with research on strategic decision making. The strength of the one used in this book lies in the fact that it reflects the ways practitioners may actually explain the outcomes of their own organizations' decisions. Such a categorization can help researchers to better understand how practitioners' theories and explanations affect their future strategic decisions. Further, attention to research topics at the interfaces between each of these perspectives may allow researchers to better assist practitioners in developing more complete explanations for strategic decisions.

Summary of Contents

Chapter 1 outlines the three major perspectives on strategic decision making. The next three chapters deal with research within each of the three perspectives on strategic decision making. The last three chapters deal with the implications of the perspectives for strategic decision aids, the use of structural conflict in combining perspectives, and the implications of these ideas for research and practice.

Chapter 2. The Rational-Choice Perspective

This chapter deals with research based on the assumption that strategic decisions are the product of intendedly rational choice and are grounded in Allison's Model I. If decisions are the outcome of conscious choice, it is of interest to know how psychological traits or tendencies influence the process of defining problems and evaluating alternatives. Research on cognitive structures and processes in strategic management addresses this question. The material in this chapter deals with the processes by which strategists may construct their models of problem situations and the factors that may affect the ways they approach the task of solving these problems.

Chapter 3. The Organizational Perspective

This chapter deals with research on the processes of strategic decision making and strategic and structural adaptation as well as the organizational factors affecting these processes. It is related to Allison's Model II. The work of strategic management researchers influenced by this model can be divided into three categories. These will be referred to as strategic decision modeling, organizational influences, and strategic and structural adaptation.

Chapter 4. The Political Perspective

Strategic management research dealing with political processes (Allison's Model III) can be divided into three categories: external sources of political power, the political structure of organizations (which relates to what Allison called "the positions"), and political maneuverings (what Allison called "the pulling and hauling"). This chapter deals with the ways these factors shape strategies.

Chapter 5. Three Types of Prescriptions for Improving
Strategic Decision Making

In this chapter, a large number of prescriptions for improving strategic decisions will be reviewed within Allison's basic framework. This chapter will clarify the basic differences between the recommendations so that they can be used more effectively. Allison's three models of the decision process can be used as a framework for explaining these differences. In actual strategic decisions, cognitive, organizational, and political processes operate simultaneously. Therefore, in this chapter, I show how the three perspectives can be combined in order to deal with the full complexity of strategic decisions.

Chapter 6. Structured Conflict and Devil's Advocacy in Strategic Decision Making

One approach to combining multiple perspectives in practice is through the principle of structured conflict. There has been a good deal of research on methods for structuring the discussion of diverse and conflicting views. This research has been summarized under the term *devil's advocacy*. This chapter deals with three basic variants of devil's advocacy. Each of these approaches is described in detail in the chapter and examples of the use of each are provided. The chapter concludes with a discussion of some rules for effective use of devil's advocacy in strategic decision making. This lays the foundation for the discussion of a conflict-based model for combining prescriptions from the cognitive, organizational, and political perspectives in the concluding chapter.

Chapter 7. Conclusion and Implications for Practice and Research

This concluding chapter discusses ways of building alternative perspectives into a strategic decision-making process. The simplified model of the decision-making process developed in chapter 5 is used as a basis for recommendations involving techniques for encouraging and managing debate between diverse alternative views of strategic problems. The chapter concludes with recommendations and questions for future research dealing with the interaction of cognitive, organizational, and political factors. Such research may assist practitioners in dealing effectively with *all* aspects of strategic problems.

This book is directed primarily toward researchers in the field of strategic management. However, since the field has a strong applied focus, and since the topics covered in the book deal with approaches to explaining decisions that may actually be used by practicing managers, the book should also have some appeal for practitioners. Researchers are encouraged to examine the recommendations for practice as *hypotheses* about effective strategic decision making that can be tested in future research.

Acknowledgments

It is impossible for me to mention everyone who contributed to my understanding of the topics covered in this book. However, there are several people who deserve explicit thanks. These include Susan Rhodes, Rick Cosier, Irene Duhaime, Jane Dutton, Anne Huff, Marjorie Lyles, Henry Mintzberg, and Howard Thomas. Although these people are not to blame for any of the book's possible faults, they should share the credit for its virtues.

1
Explaining and Improving
Strategic Decisions

S ince Peters and Waterman's book *In Search of Excellence* (1982) gave us a list of some of the "best managed companies in America," several of these excellent companies have experienced performance declines and financial difficulties. A number of articles have appeared in recent years that offer explanations for each of these companies' fall from excellence. It is interesting to examine the reasons given in these articles for particular strategic failures because they give insights into the approaches people take to explaining decision outcomes. Here, the term *strategic failures* is defined broadly to include any failure to reach important strategic or organizational goals. Such goals may be explicitly developed company-specific goals or they may be assumed generic goals of all businesses such as the avoidance of declines in profitability. I will identify three types of explanations for strategic failures given in one of these articles.

Why Do Good Companies Develop Bad Strategies?

In the November 5, 1984 issue of *Business Week,* the cover story entitled "Who's Excellent Now?" dealt with strategic failures in a number of companies identified as excellent by Peters and Waterman. The story described the recent fortunes of a group of the "excellent" companies including Atari, Delta Airlines, Digital Equip-

---

The quoted material in this chapter is reprinted from the November 5, 1984, issue of *Business Week* by special permission. ©1984 by McGraw-Hill, Inc.

ment (DEC), Hewlett-Packard, and Texas Instruments. In examining the reasons given for the strategic failures of these companies, we can identify three basic approaches to explanation. Consider the following explanation for the failure of Atari:

> Atari was so out of touch with its market that it failed to realize its customers were losing interest in video-game players and switching to home computers—a fatal oversight. (*Business Week*, 1984, p. 77)

Later in the article, Delta Airlines' slow response to deregulation was attributed to its failure to recognize the importance of computers in monitoring ticket prices (*Business Week*, 1984, p. 78). Finally, the article stated that Digital Equipment's earnings decline was due to the company's failure to foresee the increasing importance of personal computers and desktop work stations (*Business Week*, 1984, p. 86).

The reader will notice that all these explanations share a common perspective. They all seem to suggest that an organization perceives, understands, and makes decisions in ways similar to the ways an individual perceives, understands, and makes decisions. For example, Atari is said to have been guilty of an oversight; Digital Equipment experienced a failure of foresight because of the biases of the company's president. In other words, these explanations are based on the metaphor of an organization as an individual. Of course, we all realize that organizations do not have perceptions and beliefs as do individuals. However, this first perspective provides one intuitively appealing way of explaining organizational decisions and strategic failures.

Compare this first set of explanations with a second set from a different perspective. The first deals with Texas Instruments.

> An overly complex management system, including matrix management and numbers-dominated strategic planning, tended to smother entrepreneurship. TI's confusing reporting structures, for instance, delayed the design and production of key new products like large-scale computer memory chips. (*Business Week*, 1984, p. 82)

The explanation for strategic failure at Revlon focuses on the company's overreliance on modern decision-making and management techniques and systems (*Business Week,* 1984, pp. 77–78).

In these two explanations, failure is attributed to problems or inadequacies in the systems, reporting structures, and routines used to make decisions. In this perspective, the organization is viewed almost as a machine that fashions decisions through organizational processes. Strategic failures are attributed to problems and inadequacies in organizational processes or inadequate structure. Companies fail because the machinery of decision making is not working properly. Of course, no one believes an organization *literally* operates like a machine. However, this metaphor is useful in understanding the basic focus of this perspective.

The next quote, which deals with Digital Equipment's failure to achieve excellence, illustrates a third approach to explanation. The company is described as a highly politicized organization, in which "The most important thing to many managers was expanding the power of their own fiefdoms, not getting new products out the door" (*Business Week,* 1984, p. 86).

The same perspective can be seen in the explanation for Hewlett Packard's difficulties in the personal computer market. According to the article, one of the major problems was the failure of Hewlett Packard's "fiercely autonomous" divisions to cooperate with each other (*Business Week,* 1984, p. 78).

In these explanations, the organization is described using political or conflict-based metaphors and terms such as *fiefdoms.* The organization is seen as an arena in which individuals and groups compete for resources such as power, status, and money. Strategies are affected, and perhaps even determined, by this process of bargaining and conflict. Strategic failures result when powerful individuals or groups feel their interests have not been served by a new strategy. They may then block implementation.

These alternative approaches to explaining decision outcomes provide different frameworks for research on strategic decision making and for prescriptions aimed at improving strategic decisions. Following only one approach can result in a kind of narrowed focus that makes it difficult for researchers and practitioners to deal adequately with the full complexity of strategic problems. For example, those who view strategic decisions as intendedly rational attempts to reach company goals may not give sufficient attention to the organizational mechanisms or the internal political processes affecting strategic decisions. On the other hand, those who view these decisions as outcomes of political bargaining processes may not give sufficient attention to companywide goals and the ways in which strategic decisions meet these goals.

The preceding discussion of approaches to strategy formulation is not a new contribution, of course. Nor is it intended to suggest that individual prescriptions are useless. Rather, it is intended to provide the basis for a discussion of the ways such prescriptions may be intelligently used.

If we are to move beyond the prescriptions offered by single perspectives, educators in business strategy and in other business disciplines must encourage managers to think carefully and deeply about their own strategic problems and to develop their own tailormade solutions. We can assist them by providing them with summaries of the best current research on strategic decision making in readable form.

This book is an attempt to present the best current research aimed at understanding and improving strategic decision making. The framework I use to discuss this research is strongly influenced by *The Essence of Decision* (1971) by Graham Allison. As will be shown later in this chapter, the three approaches to explaining decisional failure correspond to three models for viewing decisions proposed by Allison.

What Is a Strategic Decision?

In this book, I will discuss research on strategic decisions from each of these three perspectives. Before doing this, however, it is necessary for me to define strategic decisions. The term *strategy* is widely used but difficult to define. Indeed, dozens of different definitions have been developed (Bracker, 1980), but there is no real consensus concerning which one is best. Figure 1–1 gives some of the better-known definitions.

It may not be possible to provide a brief, clear, and precise definition of strategy that encompasses all of its major elements. How-

Strategy is:

The determination of the basic long-term goals and objectives of an enterprise.

The adoption of courses of action.

The allocation of resources necessary for carrying out these goals.

Chandler (1962)

Strategy is:

Product/market scope.

Growth vector.

Competitive advantage.

Synergy.

Ansoff (1965)

Strategy is:

The pattern of objectives, purposes, or goals and major policies.

Plans for achieving these goals, stated in such a way as to define what business the company is in or is to be in and the kind of company it is or is to be.

Andrews (1971)

Strategy includes:

Scope, which may be defined in terms of product/market matches and geographic territories.

Resource deployments and distinctive competences.

Competitive advantage.

Synergy.

In three organization levels: (1) corporate, (2) business, and (3) functional.

Hofer and Schendel (1978)

Strategy:

Is the pattern of decisions in a company that shapes and reveals its objectives, purposes, or goals.

Produces the principle policies and plans for achieving these goals.

Defines the business the company intends to be in and the kind of economic and human organization it intends to be.

*Christensen, Andrews, and
Bower (1973)*

Strategy is a pattern in a stream of decisions.

Mintzberg (1978)

Figure 1–1. *Definitions of Strategy*

ever, I will try to sketch out the major characteristics of strategic decisions and to give the features that distinguish them from other types of decisions.

First, strategic decisions are *ill-structured* and *nonroutine*. Each one is somewhat unique and cannot be committed to simple decision rules. Therefore, a decision about whether to replenish inventory, which can be made using a formula, would not be a strategic decision. Digital Equipment's decision to enter the personal computer market, on the other hand, would be.

Second, strategic decisions are those that are especially *important* to an organization—those that involve large resource commitments and the possibility of large gains or losses as a result. A decision about hiring a single hourly employee would not be considered a strategic decision. However, Texas Instruments' decision to develop the home computer would be.

Finally, strategic decisions are generally very *complex*. Indeed, it is this feature that makes them interesting to study. Normative models of the strategic decision process (for example, Steiner, 1979) suggest that these decisions should be based on a consideration of broad environmental trends, competitive dynamics of an industry, company strengths and weaknesses in each functional area, and management values. Developing a strategy consistent with all these factors would be a very complex task indeed.

Three Perspectives on Strategic Decision Making

Strategic decisions can be understood through the three general models used by Allison to explain government decisions such as those made during the Cuban Missile Crisis.

In its simplest, most extreme form, Model I assumes that organizations behave as rational individuals and he explains organizations' actions on the basis of assumed goals (Allison, 1971, pp. 15–20). It is sometimes equated with Simon's notion of "economic man" who is "objectively rational" and who has *complete* knowledge of the consequences that will follow from all possible alternatives (Simon, 1976, pp. 79–84). However, as Allison points out,

there are variants on this basic model that are perhaps more realistic. In some variants, the "personality traits or psychological tendencies of the nation or government" and its "tendencies to perceive
(and to exclude) particular ranges of alternatives" are considered
(1971, pp. 36–37). The essential feature of this model is the view
of decisions as the product of intendedly rational *conscious choice.*

Allison states that in Model II, decisions are seen not as the
result of deliberate choice but as *outputs* of organizational processes. He summarizes some of the major tenets of this model. The
first is that many organizational decisions are the result of standard
operating procedures and programs. When the decision cannot be
handled by such procedures, the search of solutions follows particular *patterns* that are influenced by organizational routines. Second,
organizational adaptation produces changes in structures and routines and subsequently impacts decisions. Finally, despite the impact
of organizational processes, leaders or executives can influence the
direction of decisions. However, such influence is more limited than
complete control and can only be exercised through organizational
processes (1971, pp. 78–95).

Within Allison's Model III or "bureaucratic politics paradigm,"
decisions are seen as outcomes of political games, as "the *resultant*
of bargaining among individuals" (1971, pp. 162–180). Explaining
a decision within this model involves "displaying the game—the
action-channel, the positions, the players, their preferences, and the
pulling and hauling—that yielded, as a resultant, the action in question" (1971, p. 173).

Table 1–1 lists some of the strategic management research consistent with Allison's three models. The table does not contain all
the research relevant to each perspective. A small number of studies
have been selected for each category to clearly illustrate the thrusts
of research in each perspective.

Of course, much of the research cited in table 1–1 and the next
three chapters relates to more than one of the three perspectives. I
have focused on particular aspects of each study that relate to each
perspective.

Because many of these studies are very complex and may relate
to more than one perspective, the reader may disagree with the way
I have classified particular studies. Whether or not I have chosen

Table 1–1
Three Perspectives on Strategic Decision Making

Perspective	Theme	Root Disciplines	Representative Research
Model I: rational-choice and cognitive processes	Cognitive heuristics and biases	Cognitive psychology	Barnes (1984), Chittipeddi & Gioia (1983), Duhaime & Schwenk (1985), Hogarth (1980), Schwenk (1984a)
	Strategic assumptions	Philosophy, cognitive psychology	Mason (1969), Mason & Mitroff (1981), Freeman (1984), Shrivastava & Dutton (1983)
	Cognitive frames	Cognitive psychology	Shrivastava (1983), Chittipeddi & Gioia (1983), Gioia & Poole (1984), Shrivastava & Mitroff (1983, 1984)
	Analogy and metaphor	Cognitive psychology	Huff (1980), Isenberg (1983), Sapienza (1983), Shrivastava & Mitroff (1983)
	Individual differences	Psychology	Robey & Taggart (1981), Taggart & Robey (1981), Hambrick & Mason (1984), Miller et al. (1982), Gupta & Govindarajan (1984), Kets de Vries & Miller (1984)
Model II: organizational processes	Strategic decision modeling	Organization theory	Fahey (1981), Nutt (1984a,b), Mintzberg et al. (1976), Lyles (1981), Mazzolini (1981), Pounds (1969)
	Organizational influences	Organization theory	Steiner (1979), Quinn (1980), Banks & Wheelright (1979), Hall & Saias (1980), Burgelman (1983a,b), Fredrickson (1986)
	Strategic and structural adaptation	Organization theory, sociology	Mintzberg (1973, 1978), Miller & Friesen (1980, 1982, 1983), Mintzberg & Waters (1982), Burgelman (1983a,b), Chandler (1962)

Model III: political processes		
External sources of influence	Political science, sociology	Mintzberg (1983), Freeman (1984), Rhenman (1973), Mazzolini (1979), Sexty (1980), Murray (1978), Dirsmith & Covaleski (1983)
Internal political structure	Sociology, social psychology	Mintzberg (1983, 1984), Jemison (1984), Hickson et al. (1971), Hambrick (1981), Pfeffer (1981)
Organizational culture	Anthropology	Deal & Kennedy (1982), Peters & Waterman (1982), Pettigrew (1979), Riley (1983), Selznick (1957), Martin et al. (1983), Starbuck (1982), Dunbar et al. (1982), Brunsson (1982), Meyer (1982)
Political maneuvering	Sociology, political science	Murray (1978), Narayanan & Fahey (1982), MacMillan (1978), Quinn (1980), Farrell & Petersen (1982)

Table 1–2
Features of the Three Perspectives

	Cognitive Processes	Organizational Processes	Political Processes
Organizing concepts	Influence of cognitive structures and processes	Influence of organizational structures and processes	Influence of power and political maneuvering
Central metaphor	Organization as an intendedly rational person	Organization as a machine	Organization as a bargaining table
Rules for categorizing studies	Study deals with factors affecting problem comprehension.	Study deals with factors affecting the flow of information and decisions in organization.	Study deals with factors affecting sources and uses of power.
Questions posed by each perspective	How do cognitive sturctures, processes, and biases affect decision outcomes?	How do organizational structures and processes affect decision outcomes?	How does the distribution of power affect decision outcomes?

the correct perspective for each study is less important than the way each piece of work illustrates the features of each perspective. Table 1–2 provides, in summary form, some of the essential features of each perspective and the rules for categorizing particular studies in each perspective.

Why Use Allison's Typology?

Strategic decision researchers have proposed several typologies of the major perspectives on research in the field (Chaffee, 1985, p. 134; Jemison, 1981b; Schendel and Hofer, 1979; Mintzberg, 1978). Each of these provides a reasonable framework for the field. What are the advantages of using Allison's classification scheme?

First, Allison's models are useful because they deal with three fundamentally different perspectives for explaining large-scale organizational decisions. Allison did not simply try to develop categories in order to summarize research on decision making. He identified the three most common ways to explain decisions. As the material at the beginning of this section shows, Allison's three models correspond to three types of intuitive theories that *are* used to explain decisional failures.

Second, the use of Allison's framework suggests new research questions or directions as well as some interesting implications for practice. Since the three models deal with approaches to explanation used by practitioners *and* scholars, they may give suggestions on ways of investigating the effects of practitioners' explanatory models on the ways they attempt to improve future decisions.

The fact that Allison's three models are widely known and used provides another argument for the use of these models as a framework for the book. This acceptance is demonstrated by the fact that a number of recent researchers have found Allison's framework to be inclusive and well organized enough to form the basis of their own frameworks. Pfeffer (1981, p. 25) has developed a framework that includes Allison's three models and has suggested that there is a "decision process" perspective that is separate from the organizational process perspective. This perspective questions the assumption that there are predetermined known preferences held by organizational members. Decisions are seen as chaotic "garbage-can" processes (Cohen, March, and Olsen, 1972) that occur within "organized anarchies" (March and Olsen, 1979). In this book, this material will be treated as part of the organizational process perspective.

Chaffee (1983, pp. 5–29) has described five models of organizational decision making, including two in addition to the three proposed by Allison. She describes the garbage-can model in organized anarchies, which is covered by Pfeffer as her fourth model. In addition, she describes a collegial model in which decisions are reached through consensus. This fifth model will not be covered separately in this book. However, elements of this model will be included in the discussion of the cognitive and political perspectives.

Allison's models represent attempts to define two important alternatives to the rational-choice model. The perspectives developed in this book—the cognitive, organizational, and political perspectives—are heavily influenced by Allison's three categories. However, they are somewhat different. These differences are intended to reflect the developments in research within these categories in the time since Allison's book was written.

2

The Rational-Choice Perspective

Improving decision making is a central concern of researchers in the field of strategy. This is one reason Allison's Model I approach—which views decisions as the product of conscious choice—has dominated the field historically. The case method developed at Harvard (Christensen, Andrews, Bower, Hammermesh, and Porter, 1982) is based on the view that strategies are formulated through conscious choice by the executives who had the data described in the case.

Students in case-oriented courses are often taught to view strategy as the outcome of a *conscious decision* by top management. Further, they are encouraged to make strategic decisions themselves as a process of rational choice. Much of the text material in undergraduate and graduate policy books is designed to help students make more rational decisions. Material on organizational and political factors is usually included in strategy texts, but this material is often confined to the section on strategy implementation or a special section on social responsibility.

Guidelines for making effective strategy choices have been provided by a number of theorists from the Harvard case research tradition. Some of the best-known examples of these guidelines are provided by Andrews (1971), Ansoff (1965), and Tilles (1963).

There is a large body of research in the field that is designed to help strategists make more rational decisions. This research attempts to specify the contingencies managers should consider in formulating strategies. Since many excellent reviews of this research already exist, it will not be reviewed again in this chapter. Instead, some of the major streams of research will be identified and representative examples will be cited.

The PIMS (Profit Impact of Market Strategies) data base is managed by the Strategic Planning Institute and contains data from over 1,500 product and service businesses from over 150 companies on the factors that might affect ROI and cash flow (Schoeffler, 1977). Factors include such things as the business's market share, rate of new-product introduction, advertising expenditures, and capital intensity. Researchers using this data base have isolated factors that they feel determine strategic success (Schoeffler, 1977; Hambrick, 1983; Hambrick and Lei, 1985). This research provides general guidelines to aid managers in formulating effective strategy.

Others have studied statistical information and company histories to develop recommendations for formulating specific types of strategies in specific situations. Harrigan, for example, has developed recommendations for formulating strategies in declining businesses (1980) for vertical integration (1983) and for joint ventures (1985). Hatten, Schendel, and Cooper (1978) studied the brewing industry using the COMPUSTAT financial data base as well as other data sources and identified strategic success factors specific to this industry.

All this research is based on the assumption that executives can use this information to make rational decisions. However, the research to be discussed next suggests that cognitive limits may affect executives' attempts at rational decision making.

Cognitive Limits

The cognitive limits of key decisionmakers affect their capacity for rational strategic choice. The cognitions of key decisionmakers are receiving increased research attention in strategic management. This is due in part to the growing recognition of the importance of key decisionmakers' perceptions in studying the links between the environment, strategy, and structure.

Several studies illustrate this recognition. Lawrence and Lorsch, in their book *Organization and Environment,* choose the perceptions of top executives in three industries as the best method of defining environmental uncertainty for these industries (1969, pp. 23–30). They then use this perceptual measure as the basis for their generalization about the relationships between environment, strategy, and organizational structure. Anderson and Paine (1975) note that individual subjective factors influence environmental and organizational perceptions and, subsequently, strategy formulation. Mintzberg's (1978) distinction between *intended* and *realized* strategies underscores the importance of studying key decisionmakers' perceptions, cognitions, and intentions. Managers' perceptions and cognitions may contribute to an intended strategy bearing little resemblance to the strategy eventually realized. Researchers may be interested in the conditions under which intended strategies are not realized.

In a longitudinal study of strategic change in a retail chain, Mintzberg and Waters (1982) suggest that in the entrepreneurial mode of strategy making, the development of a new strategy is typically carried out "in a single informed brain." They conclude that this is why the entrepreneurial mode is at the center of the most glorious corporate successes (Mintzberg and Waters, 1982, p. 496). The study of strategists' cognitions provides information about the workings of these informed brains and, therefore, the factors that contribute to some glorious corporate successes (as well as some dismal strategic failures). Hambrick and Mason (1984) note that strategic decision making is influenced by the cognitive frames and decision processes of members of organizational "upper echelons."

Finally, the research on strategic issue diagnosis, problem formulation, and decision processes highlights the need for examining strategists' cognitions. (See Dutton, Fahey, and Narayanan, 1983; Lyles, 1981; Lyles and Mitroff, 1980; Mazzolini, 1981; and Mintzberg, Raisinghani, and Theoret, 1976, for a good introduction to the research on these topics.) Dutton et al. suggest that the concepts, beliefs, assumptions, and cause-and-effect understandings of strategists determine how strategic issues will be framed (1983, p. 310). Lyles notes that subjectivity is involved in the process of problem definition and suggests that strategists' problem definitions will be guided by their past experiences (1981, p. 62).

Recognizing the importance of cognitions, researchers have begun to explore their role in strategic management. In this chapter, recent research on five specific topics in strategic cognition will be summarized. These topics include cognitive heuristics and biases, cognitive frames, strategic assumptions, analogy and metaphor, and individual differences. Figure 2–1 shows the way these topics relate to each other.

The figure will be covered in detail at the end of this chapter after the individual components of the figure have been analyzed. Since much of this research is grounded in cognitive psychology and other disciplines, relevant work in these disciplines will also be considered. The chapter concludes with a discussion of issues for future research.

Research on Strategic Cognition

A useful starting point in an analysis of cognitive processes is the concept of cognitive simplification. Simon (1957, 1976) laid the groundwork for the treatment of cognitive simplification in his discussion of "bounded rationality," which suggests that decisionmak-

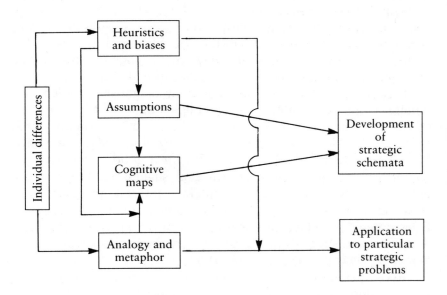

Figure 2–1. *Strategic Problem Comprehension*

ers must construct simplified mental models when dealing with complex problems (1976, pp. 79–96).

Many times, the distinction is drawn between "maximizing" and "satisficing" (finding the best solution as opposed to a merely satisfactory solution) and it is suggested that cognitive, political, and organizational factors account for decisionmakers' tendency to satisfice (Simon, 1976; Janis and Mann, 1977). However, we must go beyond the simple truth that managers often do not maximize.

Mason and Mitroff (1981) and others have observed that strategic problems are, almost by definition, extremely complex. How do strategists with limited information-processing capacities deal with this complexity in order to make sense of strategic problems? The material in the next sections deals with this question.

Attempts by strategists to understand complex problems may introduce *biases* into their *strategic assumptions*. Strategic assumptions then form the basis for the frames of reference or *schemata* through which decisionmakers represent complex strategic problems. *Analogy and metaphor* may be the means by which cognitive maps and schemata from other problem domains are applied to new strategic problems. If new strategic problems cannot be dealt with through analogy, then a complex diagnosis may have to be done. Heuristics and biases may then come into play in developing new strategic assumptions. *Individual differences* influence the ways these cognitive factors affect decision outcomes. These points will be elaborated in the research reviews that follow.

Cognitive Heuristics and Biases

The behavioral decision theory literature provides material for the study of cognitive heuristics and biases in strategic management. Researchers have recently begun to suggest that the decisional biases identified in laboratory contexts may affect strategic decision making as well (Barnes, 1984; Chittipeddi and Gioia, 1983; Schwenk, 1984d; Duhaime and Schwenk, 1985).

Extensive lists of heuristics and biases have already been developed and examples can be found in reviews by Hogarth (1980); Hogarth and Makridakis (1981); Slovic, Fischhoff, and Lichtenstein (1977); Taylor (1975); and Tversky and Kahneman (1974). Researchers have identified a number of heuristics or rules of thumb decisionmakers use to simplify complex problems and a number of decisional biases that may have an impact on strategic decisions. Tversky and Kahneman and other behavioral decision theorists have pointed out that the heuristics may provide efficient short cuts in processing information. As Tversky and Kahneman (1974, p. 1125) state, "In general, these heuristics are quite useful, but sometimes they lead to severe and systematic errors." To illustrate the nature of heuristics and biases, one example of each will be discussed here.

Strategic decisions are often influenced by judgments about the probability of certain types of changes in the environment. One heuristic that may affect such probability judgments is the *availability* heuristic (Barnes, 1984; Tversky and Kahneman, 1974). Using this heuristic, decisionmakers judge a future event to be likely if it is easy to recall past occurrences of the event. In other words, judgments of the likelihood of an event are based on the *availability* of past occurrences in memory. Generally, frequently occurring events are easier to recall than infrequently occurring events, so availability is a good way of judging probability.

However, other things besides frequency can increase the availability of certain types of events in memory. Dramatic vivid events may be easy to recall even if they occur infrequently. Also, recent events may be easier to recall. For this reason, the availability heuristic may distort judgments of probabilities.

One bias that may affect strategic decisions is the *illusion of control* (Duhaime and Schwenk, 1985; Langer, 1983; Schwenk, 1984d, 1986). This bias may affect people's assessments of their chance of success at a venture. Langer reports on six studies that show that subjects making a variety of decisions expressed an expectancy of personal success higher than the objective probability would warrant. They tend to overestimate their skill or the impact it will have on the outcome (Langer, 1983, pp. 59–90).

Langer suggests that we are subject to this illusion of personal control because of the way we collect information. She notes that as people constantly seek ways to control outcomes in the environment, they form hypotheses about the effects of their actions on these outcomes. In her words, they then "tend to seek out information that supports their hypotheses while innocently ignoring disconfirming evidence" (1983, p. 24). This type of information search tends to reinforce the illusion of personal control.

Most of the heuristics and biases have been identified in laboratory experiments using relatively structured tasks. Therefore, strategic management researchers have attempted to identify examples of the operation of the biases in actual strategic decisions. The focus on simplification processes for which laboratory *and* field support exist should increase the chance of identifying cognitive processes that really do affect organizational decisions rather than processes produced only by the artificiality of the laboratory context or the political processes in organizations. It is likely that multiple biases affect strategic decisions. Schwenk (1986) has shown how some of the biases may interact and reinforce each other. For example, the availability bias might increase the illusion of control in successful executives. These executives' past experiences of success might be salient to them and therefore more easily recalled when they are assessing their chances of success with a new strategy.

In summary, there is some evidence from the laboratory and the field that availability, the illusion of control, and other biases identified in this research may affect strategic decisions. In strategic decisions, it is likely that multiple biases operate. Researchers are now attempting to describe the ways individual biases interact to affect such decisions.

Strategic Assumptions, Cognitive Maps, and Schemata

The effects of cognitive heuristics and biases may be seen in decisionmakers' assumptions about strategic problems. Mason and Mitroff (1981) suggest that assumptions are the basic elements of a strategist's frame of reference or world view. Their book provides a good review of their research on strategic assumptions. According to Mason and Mitroff, strategic problems involve organized complexity; in other words, problem variables are interdependent in such a way that solutions to some problems create others (1981, pp. 3–21). Assumptions about such problems are necessary because policymakers must often take action in the absence of certainty

(Mason and Mitroff, 1981; Shrivastava and Dutton, 1983).

Shrivastava and Dutton (1983) give an expanded discussion of the development of strategic assumptions. Mason (1969) provides examples of strategic assumptions underlying the international expansion plan of a major abrasives manufacturing company. Three of these are provided to give a more clear idea of the nature of strategic assumptions:

1. Our competitors are quantity- and expansionist-oriented. They will cut prices.

2. Our customers are conservative and slow to change.

3. Merger opportunities are available and merger candidates are receptive.

All these assumptions deal with the behavior of groups or individuals who are important to the success of the strategy and who have a *stake* in the outcome of the strategy. Freeman (1984) calls such individuals and groups *stakeholders*. Mason and Mitroff suggest that often, "Assumptions are the characteristic properties of stakeholders that must be posited or hypothesized as premises in order to derive a strategy or policy (1981, p. 95).

Since assumptions form the basis of strategies, it is important that they be consistent with the information available to strategists. This requires careful examination of assumptions. However, this is difficult because most policymakers are unaware of the particular set of assumptions they hold and of methods that can help them in examining and assessing the strength of their assumptions (Mason and Mitroff, 1981, p. 18). The accuracy of these assumptions may be affected by the cognitive biases previously discussed.

Strategic assumptions form the basis of top managers' frames of reference. Shrivastava (1983) and Shrivastava and Mitroff (1983) suggest that analysis of these frames of reference is helpful in understanding how strategic problems are formulated. Two concepts from the cognitive psychology literature (cognitive maps and schemata) have been discussed in connection with strategic problem frames.

Cognitive Maps. The term *cognitive map* was first used by Tolman (1948) in discussions of learning in laboratory animals and human beings. These cognitive maps consist of concepts about aspects of the decision environment and beliefs about cause-and-effect-relationships between them. Such maps serve as interpretive lenses that help decisionmakers select certain aspects of an issue as important for diagnosis.

Axelrod (1976) has developed methods for representing cognitive maps diagrammatically. Though cognitive maps are often used to represent individual world views, they may be used to represent shared assumptions among a group of strategic decisionmakers. Axelrod notes that the purpose of cognitive mapping is not to represent a person's entire belief system. Rather, it represents the causal beliefs with respect to a particular decision or policy domain (Axelrod, 1976, p. 58).

These maps consist of the variables relevant to the problem with arrows linking them and plusses and minuses beside the arrows. The arrows represent causal relationships that the decisionmaker believes to exist between the variables. The plusses and minuses represent positive and negative relationships, respectively (Axelrod, 1976, pp. 55–64). Axelrod has also included a number of special symbols to represent more complex relationships and has developed mathematical rules for making predictions from them (1976, pp. 343–48).

Weick (1979) and Bougon, Weick, and Binkhorst (1977) suggest that cognitive maps may direct information search in organizations and that cognitive maps may exist at the organizational level. They are discovered or inferred by organizational members and used as a basis for action (Weick, 1979, p. 52). Cognitive maps may be derived from documents relating to particular decisions or from probing interviews with decisionmakers. Bougon (1983) provides a method called the "self-q technique" for eliciting them.

Axelrod sees cognitive maps as descriptive models that can explain the ways people actually do derive explanations of the past, make predictions of the future, and choose policies in the present (1976, pp. 56–57). He gives a number of empirical studies in the areas of foreign policy, international relations, the presidency, and the energy crisis in which cognitive maps of key decisionmakers, derived from their statements of values and causal beliefs, accurately predicted their future behavior (1976, pp. 12–14). Ford and Hegarty examined the differences between cognitive maps of MBAs and full-time practicing managers and outlined a number of future research issues dealing with cognitive mapping (1984, pp. 287–90).

Strategic choices are determined by the way strategists conceptualize their environment and industry. Cognitive mapping has proven to be a useful way of representing strategists' understanding of environmental and industry forces. Research (Shrivastava and Lim, 1984; Stubbart and Ramaprasad, 1985) has identified simplifications and biases in executives' maps of their industries. Therefore, this type of analysis might supplement research based on "objective" assessment of industry factors as determinants of strategy.

Ross (1976, pp. 96–112) has suggested that decisionmakers' cognitive maps generally contain a number of simplifications. Few goals are represented in these maps, even though multiple goals may be relevant to any particular problem. Only short paths of argument are represented even though longer chains of causality may be justified. Finally, mutual causation between variables is seldom a part of these maps. Rather, decisionmakers tend to think in terms of one-way causation.

Schemata. The term *schemata* is sometimes used in connection with cognitive maps. From the definitions of the two terms in the literature, the distinction between cognitive maps and schemata is not completely clear. In general, however, *schemata* is a broader term. A cognitive map may be defined as a particular type of schema or a part of a broader schema (Weick, 1979, pp. 48–53). Schemata have been defined as cognitive representations of attributes and the relationships between them that constitute common-sense social theories (Rumelhart and Ortony, 1977) and as active cognitive structures that frame problems (Neisser, 1976, chapter 6).

Taylor (1982, p. 72–73) and Taylor and Crocker (1983) suggest that schemata are abstract conceptions people hold about the social world, and that previously developed schemata may be applied to new problems. Chittipeddi and Gioia (1983, p. 6) state that schemata are evoked by cues in a problem-solving setting and they provide frames for problems, which make it unnecessary for decision-makers to expend the mental effort needed to completely diagnose each element of a new strategic problem.

In conclusion, human cognitive limitations introduce biases into the development of strategic assumptions and may lead to simplification in strategic schemata. These biases and simplifications affect strategic decisions when decisionmakers' existing schemata are used in diagnosing and framing new strategic problems. Analysis of executives' strategic schemata helps explain strategic choices in response to environmental and industry forces. The use of existing schemata in diagnosing new problems can be better understood through the following discussion of analogy.

Analogy in Diagnosis

In some ways, each strategic problem is unique. However, when diagnosing or framing a new strategic problem, decisionmakers may draw on their experience of situations that seem to be similar. These "similar situations" may come from relatively straightforward sources (such as previous strategic decisions) or from relatively imaginative sources (such as athletic contests). Research on analogy and metaphor in strategic decision making deals with the transfer of schemata from one domain to another.

Isenberg (1983, p. 17) has given some interesting examples of the use of metaphor and analogy in defining organizational missions and framing strategic problems. He found that managers created new meanings by comparing a current strategic issue with an issue that a prototypical organization dealt with in a particular manner. For example, a bank CEO frequently used the McDonald's hamburger chain as a way of understanding how standardization of branches could be a very powerful marketing tool. When discussing the bank's ability to compete with other banks, as well as its ability to rally its employees around a common goal, he would frequently draw an analogy to the army. The CFO of the same company would sometimes compare and contrast his control systems with those of ITT.

Isenberg also found that in order to make sense of dramatic

events, managers in a pharmaceutical company likened these events to experiences that they had already had, such as rushing at a fraternity. The process of drawing analogies seems to be very common when organizational actors are trying to understand an ambiguous or novel situation (Louis, 1980).

Analogies are more likely to shape strategic problem formulation when they are *shared* by organizational members. Sapienza (1983) has discussed the development of shared analogies that help frame strategic decisions. The process involves the creation of a shared vocabulary among the decisionmakers through discussion of problems and the emergence of shared images within the group to define the problems.

Researchers who study government decision making have insights into the uses of analogy that may be helpful to strategic management researchers. Steinbruner (1974) has discussed reasoning by analogy in foreign policy making. This involves the application of simple analogies and images to guide complex problem definition. This process helps to reduce the uncertainty perceived in the environment. Since both foreign policy and business strategy decisions are complex, ill-structured, top-level decisions, analogy may affect business strategy as well.

Reasoning by analogy has been shown to be effective in generating creative solutions to a variety of problems (Gordon, 1961). However, in strategic decisions, which involve a great deal of uncertainty and complexity, the use of simple analogies may mislead the decisionmakers into an overly simplistic view of the situation (Steinbruner, 1974, p. 115). When decisionmakers use analogies to define problems, they may not recognize that there are critical differences between their analogies and the decision situations they face.

The past often provides a ready source of analogies. Present decisions may be viewed as similar to past decisions (Huff, 1982, p. 123). May (1973) in his book, *"Lessons" of the Past* notes that foreign policy decisionmakers frame present problems by using analogies to the past. They sometimes select the first analogy that comes to mind rather than searching more widely or pausing to analyze the case and ask in what ways it might be misleading (May, 1973, p. xi). Gilovich (1981) demonstrated that analogies to the past influenced decisionmakers' recommendations about how to resolve a hypothetical international relations crisis in a laboratory experiment. Subjects developed different recommendations depending on whether the scenario they received had information suggesting similarities to World War II or to Vietnam.

Huff (1982) notes that a firm may also draw on the analogous experiences of other firms in the industry. She suggests that this may account for the similarities in strategic concepts and frames among firms in a single industry.

In summary, diagnosis of a strategic problem sometimes involves the application of a relevant schema from another domain. Essentially, the decisionmaker draws an analogy between the causes and solutions for the current problem and those of past problems. Analogies then specify the ways the problem should be solved, particularly if they are shared by organizational members. Individuals' past experiences and the experiences of other companies in the industry provide the most common sources of analogy.

Individual Differences

In addition to studying basic cognitive processes and structures common to all strategists, some researchers have focused on individual differences that may affect the way strategists approach, define, and solve strategic problems. In the final section of this chapter, I shall discuss research on three basic categories of variables dealing with individual differences: cognitive style, demographic factors, and personality traits.

Cognitive Style. An executives' cognitive style determines the way he or she approaches problems. Robey and Taggart (1981) and Taggart and Robey (1981) provide a basic description of the concept of cognitive style and the means of measuring it. They suggest that there are three basic approaches to the measurement of cognitive style: those based on physiological indicators, those based on observed behavior, and those based on self-description.

Demographic Factors. Hambrick and Mason (1984) have discussed a number of demographic factors that should affect strategic decision outcomes. They note that strategic decision making is influenced by the cognitive frames and decision processes of members of organizational "upper echelons." Anecdotal evidence in the business press supports this view. Business ventures (particularly if they fail) are often described as being the result of the predispositions and thought processes of key upper-level decisionmakers. Hambrick and Mason do not deal directly with cognitions, so their work is not included in the summaries that follow. However, they identify a number of decisionmaker characteristics that should be related to differences in cognitions and that should explain some of the variance in strategic choices. These characteristics include age, education, socioeconomic roots, and career experience.

Personality Traits. Several studies have dealt with the effects of personality traits on various types of strategic decisions. Miller, Kets de Vries, and Toulouse (1982) examined the relationship between the strategies pursued by a group of thirty-three firms and the locus of control of the firms' senior executives. Locus of control was measured using a scale developed by Julian Rotter. This scale measures individuals' perceptions of how much control they have over outcomes in their lives. Those who believe fate or luck controls outcomes are called externals. Those who believe they themselves control outcomes are called internals (Miller et al., 1982, p. 238).

Miller et al. found correlations between top executives' loci of control and their self-reports on a number of elements of their companies' strategies. Companies managed by more internal executives tended to pursue more innovative strategies, engaged in more new-product R&D, and made more dramatic changes to their product lines.

Gupta and Govindarajan (1984) collected information on the personality traits of a sample of fifty-eight strategic business unit (SBU) managers and the intended strategies of the SBUs they managed as well as their success in implementing these SBU strategies. They found that SBU managers with greater marketing and/or sales experience, greater willingness to take risk, and higher tolerance for ambiguity tended to be more successful at implementing "build" strategies but not "harvest" strategies (1984, pp. 37–38).

Kets de Vries and Miller (1984) have taken a psychoanalytic approach to the examination of personality types and their effect on strategy. In this book, they describe organizations in terms of five common neurotic styles identified in the psychoanalytic literature: paranoid, compulsive, dramatic, depressive, and schizoid.

Integration and Questions for Future Research

The previous sections summarize research on five major streams of research on strategic cognitions. These have yet to be integrated into an overall theory of cognition in strategic choice. In this final section, an integrative model is proposed and a number of future research questions are developed from this model.

Though the relationships between the research streams within the cognitive perspective have not yet been articulated, they can be integrated around two basic concepts: the development of schemata and the application of schemata to the diagnosis of particular strategic problems. Figure 2–1 describes the relationships between the four types of strategic cognitions and the two processes of schemata development and application.

This model is based on the assumption that there are two basic ways in which understanding of strategic problems is achieved. First, in order to comprehend some types of strategic problems, data may be carefully analyzed and a new schema may be *developed*. For other types of problems, understanding may be achieved by *applying* a previously developed schema to the current strategic problem. This involves less diagnosis and information search.

Mintzberg, Raisinghani, and Theoret (1976) have discussed similar ideas in connection with the development of *solutions* to strategic problems. They suggest that, in some cases, solutions are designed to deal with very new strategic problems. In other cases, preexisting solutions developed for other problems are sought out and applied to the problem. Mintzberg et al. suggest that two fundamentally different thought processes underlie the activities of design and search (1976, pp. 255–56).

In the model in figure 2–1, individual differences influence the development of heuristics and biases that affect the development of strategic assumptions and cognitive maps that, in turn, affect the development of strategic schemata. The term *schemata,* being a broader term than *cognitive maps,* is used to describe the basic cognitive structures through which strategic problems are understood. Schemata may contain cognitive maps as well as assumptions about the strength of the relationship between variables, assessments about decisionmakers' degree of confidence, and so forth. Cognitive heuristics and biases may affect the development of cognitive maps. Analogy is the means by which previously developed schemata are applied to new strategic problems. These processes are described in more detail in the following discussions on the development and application of schemata.

The Development of Schemata

Simon's work (1957, 1976) suggests that schemata are *simplified* models of the relationships between variables relevant to a strategic problem. Given the complexity of strategic problems and the cognitive limitations of strategists, some types of simplification are needed. Heuristics and biases may enter into this simplification process. Individuals may be more or less susceptible to these biases, while variables such as cognitive style, personality traits, and demographic factors may help explain these differences.

Researchers have not yet dealt explicitly with the *types* of biases that might affect the development of strategic assumptions and cognitive maps. However, work on the availability heuristic suggests that strategists' judgments about the causal relationships between variables in their cognitive maps would be distorted by their recollections of vivid events. Research on the illusion of control suggests that the causal role of key individuals would be exaggerated in strategists' cognitive maps. The role of environmental variables, which are difficult to control, would be underestimated.

An example of the presence of bias in cognitive maps will serve to clarify these points. Huff and Schwenk (1986) constructed cognitive maps from public statements explaining company performance by executives of Exxon during years of good and poor financial performance from 1973 to 1980. They found that cognitive maps that explain poor performance contain significantly more assumptions about the environment while those that explain good performance contain more assumptions dealing with the effects of executives' actions.

These differences can be explained in terms of the biases that might affect the development of these maps. The illusion of control may explain why executives focus on their own actions when identifying the causes of good performance. Executives may believe that they are in control of their companies and that the actions they take will improve performance. When performance is good, this reinforces their perception that they are in control and leads them to explain performance in terms of their own actions.

In bad years, executives must explain, to themselves and others, the factors that caused performance to decline despite their best efforts. They would tend to focus on external environmental factors over which they had relatively little control. These factors would be more salient to them. The availability heuristic would lead them to focus on these factors in developing their cognitive maps to explain performance.

The previous speculations on the effects of cognitive heuristics and biases on strategic assumptions and cognitive maps provide the basis for several questions for future research.

Which of the biases identified in previous research have the most impact on strategic assumptions?

How do cognitive heuristics and biases affect the choice of variables for inclusion in cognitive maps?

How do heuristics and biases affect the incorporation of conflicting strategic assumptions into cognitive maps?

Do individual differences affect decisionmakers' susceptibility to particular heuristics and biases?

Analogy and metaphor may affect the development of cognitive maps dealing with strategic issues. Cognitive maps deal with variables and the causal relationships between them. Analogy and metaphor may suggest causal relationships to decisionmakers developing new cognitive maps. For example, referring to figure 2–1, strategists attempting to determine the effect of new-product introduction on competitors' behavior may draw on analogies to other industries with which they are familiar (Huff, 1982). Or, they may draw on analogies to the past (May, 1973) or to competitive games and sports or other personal experiences (Isenberg, 1983).

The use of analogies was apparent in the cognitive maps of the Exxon executives (Huff and Schwenk, 1986). For example, in the late 1970s, the future behavior of the OPEC nations was discussed in terms of analogies to their past behavior. Sometimes the company's own actions were justified by citing analogous actions by other companies in the industry.

These considerations suggest some questions for future research on the effects of analogy and metaphor on cognitive maps.

What are the most common sources of analogies used in the construction of cognitive maps?

How do differences in strategists' personal experiences and industry experiences affect their choice of analogies?

The Application of Schemata

If a broad definition of the term *analogy* is adopted, it could be said that *any* application of a previously developed schema to a new strategic problem involves analogy. Analogy and metaphor may be the basic processes by which schemata are transferred from one domain to another.

Those writing an analogy and metaphor have not clearly specified the cognitive processes by which they affect strategic problem comprehension. However, it appears that cognitive heuristics and biases may be involved in this process. For example, the *availability* heuristic might cause decisionmakers to use dramatic and vivid events as the basis for their problem-defining analogies, even though these events may bear little resemblance to the problems they are attempting to understand. The *illusion of control* bias may lead decisionmakers to use analogies to situations in which they had a great deal of control over outcomes, even though this may not be true of the present situation. Further, this bias may draw decision-makers' attention to aspects of the strategic problem over which they have control. These aspects of the problem then provide the *cues* used in selecting an analogy.

An example to illustrate these points comes from the DeLorean Motor Company (Bateman and Schwenk, 1986; Levin, 1983). One of the major decisional errors John DeLorean made was to push production to 20,000 automobiles per year and later to 30,000 per year against the recommendations of his entire management team (Levin, 1983, p. 280). However, analogies to his experiences at General Motors apparently directed his thinking about the best way to build automobiles. At GM, DeLorean developed schemata relevant to all aspects of the production and sale of automobiles. There were, of course, numerous differences between GM and the new DeLorean Motor Company. However, DeLorean did not use appropriate caution in drawing on his experiences at GM. He claimed that the DeLorean plant was scaled to produce efficiently at 25,000 to 30,000 units per year—a practice that would have been more reasonable at GM than for a new company (Levin, 1983, p. 281). However, DeLorean was convinced that the company would be able to sell all the cars produced, despite the fact that a report from marketing research consultants J.D. Powers and Associates indicated that the company would be able to sell only about 4,000 automobiles per year at their price of $28,000 (Levin, 1983, p. 281).

It may be that the illusion of control nurtured by DeLorean's string of dramatic and vivid successes at GM made him less cautious in using analogies to his experiences there. Since many of these experiences were highly positive, the availability bias may also have come into play.

These points lead to two questions for further research:

Which of the biases identified in previous research has the most impact on the use of analogy and metaphor in strategic problem comprehension?

How do individual differences affect which *cues* are used in selecting an appropriate analogy?

Conclusion

In this chapter, I have surveyed recent research on five specific topics related to strategic cognitions. I have also developed a model that shows the interrelationships between these topics and I have provided an example to illustrate the features of this model.

As was stated at the beginning of the chapter, interest in strategic cognitions is growing because of increased awareness of their role in strategic-issue diagnosis and problem formulation. Research on cognitive structures, processes, and biases gives insights into the ways decisionmakers with limited cognitive capacities comprehend and solve very complex strategic problems. It may also give insights into the types of errors they commit in strategic decision making. However, no one has yet shown how these separate streams of research relate to each other. Such integration is necessary in order for future research to provide a complete understanding of strategic problem solving. There are still a number of questions about these connections that should be addressed by future research. Some of these questions were listed in the previous section.

Research on these questions should be based on detailed interviews, meetings transcripts, and other data sources containing direct information about the way strategists define strategic problems. It will be exploratory and will probably involve primarily qualitative rather than quantitative research methodologies.

As Schwenk (1985c) has pointed out, a basic assumption underlying this research is that cognitive structures and processes of key decisionmakers explain a significant portion of the variance in strategic decision outcomes. The validity of this assumption depends on the characteristics of the organization and the power configuration of the decision-making group. In those decision-making situations where a single individual or cohesive group dominates, cognitive processes are more likely to influence organizational decisions (Schwenk, 1984d). Fredrickson (1984) has suggested that centralization may increase the impact of cognitions on decisions. Further work of this type will be useful in specifying the conditions under which cognitions could be expected to shape strategic decision outcomes.

A better understanding of strategists' cognitive structures and processes will also provide a basis for better recommendations for improving strategic decision making. Strategic decision aids can be developed that are more consistent with the ways decisionmakers represent strategic problems. Also, once the most important biases are identified, decision aids can be designed to reduce these. Decision aids may also be developed to help decisionmakers more carefully examine the analogies they use to define new problems.

3
The Organizational Perspective

In the previous chapter, I discussed research based on the assumption that strategic decisions are the result of intendedly rational choices. However, strategic decisions can also be seen as the result of organizational characteristics, as in Allison's Model II. Some of the research in strategic management deals with the effects of organizational processes and structure. Thus, it is consistent with Allison's Model II.

Allison states that in this model, decisions are seen not as the result of deliberate choice as in Model I, but as *outputs* of organizational processes. This perspective has its roots in organization theory, a young discipline, which can be traced back to works such as Barnard's *The Functions of the Executive* (1938) and Simon's *Administrative Behavior* (1976). Works by March and Simon (1958) and Cyert and March (1963) helped outline the major features of this perspective.

Few researchers in strategic management would argue that organizational processes, programs, and structures *determine* strategic decision outcomes. However, all would agree that these factors can *influence* strategic decision making. Researchers within this perspective provide information on these factors through the study of patterns in strategic decision making and strategic and structural adaptation.

Strategic management researchers have devoted a good deal of attention to three topics that are consistent with Allison's organizational processes perspective. The first deals with what Allison would call the patterns in the search for solutions. Many

---

Some of the material in the "Strategic Decision Modeling" section of this chapter appeared in an earlier paper in *Academy of Management Review*, 1985, *10*, 496–503.

researchers have attempted to develop models of strategic decision processes and to identify the major types of decision processes.

The second topic deals with the ways in which organizational systems (for example, evaluation and reward systems and strategic planning systems) and structures may influence strategic decisions. This research helps provide insights into the organizational factors that may determine the characteristics of decision processes within a firm.

The third major topic deals with the process of strategic and structural adaptation to environmental change. Rather than focusing on single strategic decisions, researchers in this area deal with large-scale adaptation that may involve many individual strategic and structural changes.

Figure 3–1 shows the relationship between these topics and their relationship to individual strategic decisions. The figure will

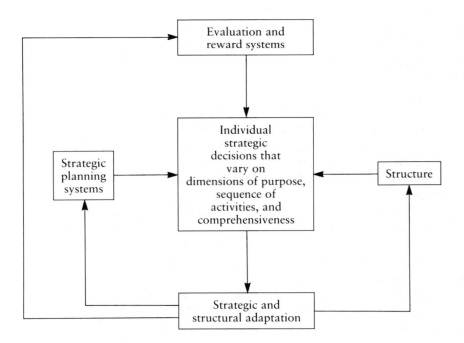

Figure 3–1. *Effects of Organizational Factors on Strategic Decisions*

be discussed in detail after the individual topics have been discussed.

Strategic Decision Modeling

Research on this topic deals with the ways problem-solving activity is structured in decisions involving multiple participants and long time frames. Many researchers have found that decisional activity occurs in stages (such as problem formulation, solution generation, and choice) with a great deal of cycling between stages (Lyles, 1981; Mintzberg, Raisinghani, and Theoret, 1976; Nutt, 1984a, 1984b; Pounds, 1969). However, some organizational theorists have questioned the existence of stages and have portrayed the decision process as rather chaotic and purposeless (Schwenk, 1985b).

Participants' recollections are frequently used data sources in the study of organizational decision-making processes. Archival data and field observation are of limited use because the organizational decision process often leaves few traces in organizational records and because outside observers who are not familiar with the details of a decision cannot draw sufficient information from their observations to generate an accurate model of the process.

One defining characteristic of models based on participant recollection is the assumption that decision making occurs in phases— that at any one point in the decision process, a particular type of decisional activity dominates all the others. Another important feature of these models is that decision making is *purposeful* and *goal-directed*.

Numerous researchers have elicited decisionmakers' descriptions of organizational decisions in which they were involved. Descriptive models of the decision-making process developed through participant recollection are typically sequential and contain varying numbers of stages or phases as well as feedback loops allowing decisional activity to cycle between phases. To illustrate the characteristics of these models, a number of examples will be reviewed in this section of the chapter.

The examples cited do not constitute an exhaustive list of the decision process models in the literature. A detailed review of alternative organizational decision process models is beyond the scope of this chapter. However, discussions of the major alternative models may be found in earlier reviews (Allison, 1971; Etzioni, 1967; Lang, Dittrich, and White, 1978).

Pounds (1969) used data obtained primarily from interviews with organizational decisionmakers to construct his classic model of the problem-finding/problem-solving process. This model contains the following phases with the specification that decisional activity can recycle from the last to the first phase (Pounds, 1969, p. 6):

1. Choose a model.

2. Compare it to reality.

3. Identify differences.

4. Select a difference.

5. Consider alternative operators.

6. Evaluate consequences of operators.

7. Select an operator.

8. Execute the operator.

Pounds indicated that, in addition to using participant recollection, he also observed meetings during which problems were identified. However, this observation of meetings was done primarily to supplement the interview data.

Mintzberg et al. (1976) developed a sequential and cyclical model of the organizational decision-making process that involved heavy emphasis on problem identification, diagnosis, and formulation. Their model involves the following phases and routines:

A. *The Identification Phase*

　　1. *The Decision Recognition Routine:* Opportunities, problems, and crises are recognized and evoke decisional activity.

　　2. *The Diagnosis Routine:* Information relevant to opportuni-

ties, problems, and crises is collected and problems are more clearly identified.

B. *The Development Phase*

3. *The Search Routine:* Organizational decisionmakers go through a number of activities to generate alternative solutions to problems.

4. *The Design Routine:* Ready-made solutions that have been identified are modified to fit the particular problem or new solutions are designed.

C. *The Selection Phase*

5. *The Screen Routine:* This routine is activated when the search routine generates more alternatives than can be intensively evaluated. Alternatives are quickly scanned and the most obviously infeasible are eliminated.

6. *The Evaluation-Choice Routine:* An alternative is chosen through either a process of analysis and judgment or a process of bargaining among decisionmakers.

7. *The Authorization Routine:* When the individual making the decision does not have the authority to commit the organization to a course of action, the decision must move up the organizational hierarchy until it reaches a level at which the necessary authority resides.

Further, the model describes cyclic processes by which decisionmakers may return to earlier phases as necessary. Dynamic factors in the decision environment may delay or speed up the decision process or may force decisionmakers to repeat cycles (Mintzberg et al., 1976).

Later research using participant recollection has confirmed and expanded upon these sequential cyclical models. A study by Lyles (1981) involved interviews of thirty-three business executives and yielded a sequential and cyclical model focusing on the decision recognition and diagnosis routines of the identification phase. Lyles' model includes the substages of awareness/incubation, triggering, information gathering, and resolution, as well as numerous feedback loops. Fahey (1981), in a study of energy management decisions in large multidivisional firms, found three main phases involving (1) establishment of overall corporate goals and objectives, (2) development of detailed divisional plans, and (3) development of implementation programs. Nutt (1984a), in his study of decision-making processes in service agencies, identified the phases of formulation conceptualization, detailing, evaluation, and implementation. Though individual decisionmakers may not all be engaged in the same decisional activity at the same time, these phases describe the main focus of organizational activity at any point in time.

Witte (1972), Cohen, March, and Olsen (1972), and Anderson (1983) have developed alternative models based on archival data, field observation, and analyses of transcripts of meetings. These bear little resemblance to the types of models previously discussed. There are two major differences between decision process models based on participant recollection and those based on archival records, meeting transcripts, or field observations.

The first difference between the two types of models has to do with the nature or the "how" of the decision-making process. Models such as those of Pounds (1969), Mintzberg et al. (1976), and Lyles (1981) describe the decision process as involving a number of distinct phases. In the words of Mintzberg et al., "We find logic in delineating distinct phases of the decision process but not in postulating a simple sequential relationship between them" (1976, p. 252). Those who have developed these recollection-based models do not claim that organizational decision making is simple or orderly. Mintzberg et al., for example, have pointed out the complexity and ill-structuredness of such decisions. In place of a simple sequential relationship, the authors describe a process involving feedback cycles, interrupts, and numerous subroutines. However, this model and the other models previously discussed are phase models because they imply (1) that one type of activity dominates others at any point in the decision process and (2) that decisionmakers' attention is focused on one phase at a time.

These models are contradicted by the work of Witte (1972), which was based on examination of records of company correspondence with regard to the decision to purchase electronic data processing systems. He found no evidence that decisionmakers focused on one particular kind of decisional activity at any point in the decision process. Instead, four major types of decisional activities (information gathering, alternatives development, alternative evaluation, and alternative selection) occurred *simultaneously,* with approximately equal frequency, throughout the decision process. The total level of activity was high at the beginning of the process and at the end, just prior to choice, with a relatively low level of activity between these points. Witte suggests that decisionmakers cannot gather information without simultaneously developing *and* evaluating alternatives (Witte, 1972, p. 180).

A similar conclusion is supported by Anderson's (1983) analysis of four meetings of the Executive Committee of the National Security Council attempting to deal with the 1963 Cuban Missile Crisis. Anderson classified each of the statements made at the meetings into one of thirteen categories. Some of these were similar to the categories used in Witte's study: task description, goal specification, alternatives generation, and decision. The results of Anderson's analysis show no evidence for the "phase theorem" that one type of decisional activity dominated at any one stage. Thus, the results are consistent with those of Witte's analysis.

The second major difference between decision models based on participant recollection and those based on other data sources has to do with the purposefulness or the "why" of the decision-making process. Mintzberg and others, through their flowchart models, imply that decisional activity occurs in a sequence and that the purpose of development activities such as information gathering and alternatives generation is to reach a decision. This implies that the process is goal-directed and purposeful.

However, there are alternative models of the organizational choice process that do not assume that the process is purposeful. Cohen, March, and Olsen's (1972) Garbage Can model of choice is perhaps the clearest statement of this alternative type of model. This model is also dealt with and elaborated in works by March and Simon (1958), Cyert and March (1963), Cohen and March (1974), Simon (1976), March and Olsen (1979), and Feldman and March (1981). Though it is not necessary to attempt a full explanation of the Garbage Can model in this chapter, some of its basic features will be discussed in order to show how it contrasts with models assuming that decision making is a purposeful process.

In describing the choice process in an "organized anarchy," the authors construct a model involving independent streams of *problems* that persist through time, potential solutions and solution technologies that evolve, and decisionmakers who are seeking a useful way to employ their time. Organizational choice is seen as the almost random convergence of "several relatively independent streams within an organization" (Cohen et al., 1972, p. 3), of "choice looking for problems, issues and feelings looking for decision situations in which they might be aired, solutions looking for issues to which they might be an answer, and decisionmakers looking for work" (Cohen et al., 1972, p. 1).

It is possible for development activities such as information gathering, alternatives generation, and alternatives evaluation to continue for long periods of time. However, solution of the problem only becomes possible after a choice opportunity emerges through the almost random meeting of these three streams (Cohen et al., 1972, p. 16). In such a process, it is possible for development activity to occur without being followed by choice. Further, a number of problems may become attached to a particular choice opportunity with the result that the final choice may only partially resolve the problem that was the subject of the development activity.

Anderson (1983) provides a list of the types of alternatives proposed during meeting 6 of the Ex Comm group that shows that the group did not simply consider competing alternatives for achieving a prespecified goal. Rather, they proposed numerous alternatives during the course of the decision that were decided upon individually and that actually served to help decisionmakers discover and define goals. He states, "[In the rational model] identifying goals is the first step in making a decision. On the basis of the records of the Ex Comm's deliberations, a more accurate description is that goals are discovered in the course of making a decision" (Anderson, 1983, p. 211).

The decision began with a broad recognition that the placement of missiles posed a problem. This broad negotiation could, in a sense, be called a global goal. However, specific goals to be achieved by U.S. action (goals having to do with influencing world opinion, preserving the maximum number of future options, and making use of U.S. naval superiority) were discovered during the process of debate on specific alternatives. In Anderson's words, "Goals are discovered through argumentation and debate" (Anderson, 1983, p. 213). Thus, the process of decision making was not purposeful in the sense that decisionmakers attempted to reach preestablished goals.

It may be that strategic decision processes are *both* structured and chaotic. In other words, these processes may be fundamentally chaotic with a phase structure *imposed* on them in order to coordinate the activities of multiple decisionmakers. In any process involving multiple participants, it is likely that some may be involved in one type of decisional activity while others are involved in other types. However, a loose structure corresponding to a phase model may be imposed on the process by the individual or group responsible for the final decision to ensure that the decision is made "rationally." Individuals who are asked to recall the decision process may recall this basic structure and may tend to forget actions taken by individuals on aspects of the decision process that do not fit with the basic model. In any case, it seems reasonable that the activities identified in the phase models actually occur, though they may not occur in a particular order.

Researchers studying strategic decision processes have also sought to identify the factors that contribute to *differences* in decision processes. The complexity of the decision (Fahey, 1981), the novelty of the decision (Fahey, 1981; Nutt, 1984b), and the categorization of the initial decision stimulus as either a problem or an opportunity (Mintzberg et al., 1976) have been shown to affect the type and amount of decisional activity that occurs.

Many researchers have called for more research into the *initial* phases of decision-making activity that have been called problem finding (Pounds, 1969), problem formulation (Lyles, 1981; Mintzberg et al., 1976), and issue diagnosis (Dutton, Fahey, and Narayanan, 1983). Though these are the decisional activities that are most difficult to study, they are also the activities that have the greatest impact on the range of alternatives considered and the final choice (Lyles, 1981; Mintzberg et al., 1976).

The research previously discussed deals with the *process* of strategic decision making. The next section deals with organizational factors that may influence this process.

Organizational Influences

The research discussed in this section deals with some of the organizational factors that may influence strategic decision processes and outcomes. Specifically, this section will focus on the effects of organizational systems and structure on strategic decision outcomes. There has been much speculation about the effects of planning systems, control systems, and evaluation and reward systems on strategic decision outcomes. Unfortunately, empirical research supporting these speculations is somewhat more rare.

Some research suggests that formal planning may have positive effects on strategic decision making, which in turn produces better performance (Robinson, 1982). However, research on the relationship between planning and performance has not produced consistent results (Schrader, Taylor, and Dalton, 1984). It may be that a direct and specific examination of the effects of planning on decision-making patterns would shed light on the conflict in past research results.

The use of formal planning systems is related to the issue of comprehensiveness in strategic decision making. Some researchers have argued that formal strategic planning systems improve strategic decision making by rendering it more comprehensive, systematic, and thorough (Steiner, 1979). However, others have suggested that formal planning may inhibit innovative strategy making and therefore reduce the quality of strategic decisions (Quinn, 1980). Fredrickson (1984) and Fredrickson and Mitchell (1984) have questioned the value of comprehensive decision processes. These authors report on two studies in which executives read scenarios describing hypothetical companies' problems and answered a questionnaire on the decision processes their companies would use to analyze and solve these problems. For companies in an unstable industry, they found a negative relationship between the executives' reports on the comprehensiveness of their companies' decision processes and the economic performance of the companies (Fredrickson and Mitchell,

1984). However, Fredrickson found a positive relationship for companies in a stable industry (Fredrickson, 1984).

The effects of evaluation and reward systems on strategic thinking have also been discussed (Banks and Wheelwright, 1979). It is often suggested that reward systems that focus on short-term profits discourage long-term strategic thinking. More detailed examination of decision processes in companies with different reward systems might help to confirm these assertions.

The impact of structure on strategic decision making has received more attention. Hall and Saias (1980) have noted that structure may influence strategic decision outcomes by conditioning the perceptions of organizational members and by impeding the development of planning systems. Burgelman (1983, 1983b) has described the ways structure can be manipulated in order to shape strategy. Burgelman (1983a) discussed the relationship between structural change and new-venture creation. In a field study of internal corporate venturing in a diversified major firm, he assessed the ways corporate-level management manipulated the structural context to influence the process of new-venture development (Burgelman, 1983b).

Fredrickson (1986) has discussed the possible effects of three structural variables (centralization, formalization, and complexity) on characteristics of the strategic decision process. He identifies six basic characteristics of the strategic decision process that may be affected by structural factors. These decision process characteristics include: (1) how and where the decision process is initiated (is the process initiated by problems, opportunities, or crises, and do high-level or low-level organizational members assume responsibility for initiating the process?); (2) the role of the goals (whose goals and what type of goals are served by the decision-making process?); (3) the relationship between means and ends (will the means available to achieve goals have a significant impact on the goals themselves?); (4) the explanation of strategic actions (what will be the impact of organizational and political processes on the decision outcome?); (5) the comprehensiveness of the decision-making process (what factors pose the primary constraints on comprehensiveness?); (6) the comprehensiveness in integrating decisions (what is the level of integration achieved?). Fredrickson has developed twelve propositions about the effects of centralization, formalization and complexity on the strategic decision process. These propositions, for the most part, have yet to be empirically tested. Research on the effects of systems and structure on strategic decision making has been rather sparse. Indeed, the topics dealt with in this section represent some of the most promising areas for future research.

However, at this point, it is possible to develop some generalization about how structure should influence strategic decisions based on Fredrickson's propositions. Structure conditions the perceptions of organizational decisionmakers and may make certain approaches to decision making more likely. The greater the centralization in any organization, the greater the likelihood that the decision process will be proactive and intendedly rational. The greater the level of formalization, the greater the likelihood that the decision process will be incremental and follow standard operating procedures. The greater the complexity, the greater the likelihood that the decision will be the result of bargaining processes (Fredrickson, 1986, p. 284).

In summary, the planning, evaluation and reward systems, and structure of a company may affect its strategic decision processes. Having reviewed this material, it is appropriate to consider the strategic and structural adaptation process next.

Strategic and Structural Adaptation Processes

Numerous individual strategic decisions shape a business's strategic posture. Though individual strategic decisions may be intendedly rational and goal-directed, the overall adaptation process may occur without overriding goals, in an incremental fashion (Quinn, 1980). If overriding goals do exist, they may form the basis for top management's *intended* strategy. However, during the adaptation process, the strategy is modified. The final *realized* strategy may be quite different from the intended strategy (Mintzberg, 1978, pp. 945–46). Here, the term *adaptation* refers to changes in strategy and structure that serve to improve a company's fit with its environment.

Quinn (1980) provides a description of the process of adaptation through "logical incrementalism." Drawing on the work of Lindblom (1959), Quinn examined strategic change in a number of well-managed firms and concluded that they used a "different subsystem to formulate strategy for each major class of strategic issue" (1980, p. 18). Quinn's work suggests that individual decision processes of the type Mintzberg et al. (1976) describe represent individual streams of activity that combine to form an overall strategy for a firm.

Strategic adaptation does not occur as a smooth process. New environmental demands may be dealt with temporarily by small-scale changes in procedures. After periods of relative stability, discontinuous, "revolutionary" changes in the firm's basic strategy occur (Miller and Friesen, 1980, 1983).

Mintzberg and Waters (1982) draw on earlier work by Mintzberg (1978) in their description of the process of strategic change in a Canadian grocery chain. Over several decades, this organization's approach to strategy making shifted from an entrepreneurial mode, in which strategy making was dominated by a strong leader to a planning mode dominated by formal analysis. Their results support Miller and Friesen's contention that major changes in strategies occur relatively infrequently in "sprints" with relatively long "pauses" between sprints (1982, p. 493).

Changes in organizational structure sometimes follow changes in strategy (Chandler, 1962). Chandler's pioneering work has influenced all recent research on this topic. As firms grow and their strategies become more complex, their structures tend to become more differentiated. Mintzberg and Waters demonstrated this point in their discussion of the structural changes accompanying growth in a retail chain (1982, pp. 478–79). They found that the company's structure evolved from a simple informal structure through functional departmentalization with increasing elaboration of hierarchy and support staff, through complete divisionalization.

However, structural changes do not always occur in small increments. Miller and Friesen (1982), using questionnaire data from Canadian and Australian firms and published case histories of U.S. firms, examined different types of structural changes. They used this data to test propositions about the relative effectiveness of quantum versus piecemeal-incremental approaches to change. Their conclusions were that successful firms generally were found to have a significantly higher percentage of extreme (quantum) changes along structural variables than were unsuccessful firms. . . . Incremental structural change was less likely to be undertaken by high performing firms" (1982, p. 890).

In conclusion, the work of these researchers shows that strategic and structural adaptation to environmental change is not a smooth process. Organizational inertia works against frequent change. This organizational inertia results from the expense and difficulty involved in changing established procedures, systems, and structures. Indeed, the results of the Miller and Friesen (1982) study suggest that large-scale quantum changes rather than small-scale incremental changes may be associated with higher levels of organizational performance. It may be that the most effective way to overcome organizational inertia is through frequent large-scale changes.

These results conflict to some extent with some normative prescriptions that suggest relatively frequent strategic and structural changes to deal with environments that change rapidly. Such frequent changes may be disruptive to companies and may actually result in lower performance. Recommendations for frequent changes in strategic orientation do not place sufficient importance on the organizational factors and constraints identified within the organizational perspective.

Conclusion

All the research discussed in this chapter deals with *organizational processes* by which strategic decisions are made, the factors that influence these decision processes, and the ways these processes shape strategic and structural adaptation. Thus, they are consistent with the organizational processes model.

Figure 3–1 shows the relationship between the streams of research summarized in this chapter. Strategic planning systems, evaluation and reward systems, and organizational structure all affect the process of strategic decision making. The combination of individual strategic decisions produces overall strategic and structural adaptation. This adaptation, in turn, should produce changes in planning, evaluation, and reward systems.

Questions about the relationship between the elements in the model can only be addressed when basic questions about the nature of the strategic decision process have been answered. Is the process fundamentally purposeful and sequential or not?

Approaches must be developed for combining data from various sources in such a way that they challenge and improve upon models developed through a single data source, rather than merely confirming and slightly extending them. Two recommendations for the effective use of multiple data sources in the study of organizational decision processes can be offered. These are discussed next.

One recommendation is that numerous researchers should be involved in the study of a particular decision and that each one should deal with a particular data source (One might develop a model based on managers' recollections while another independently develops a model based on meetings transcripts or other archival data.) Different decision process models might emerge from different data sources. Discussion of the points of difference between researchers could lead to richer final models as well as interesting insights about the reasons for differences that emerge from alternate views of "the same" decision process.

In decisions where documentation is sparse and participants' recollection provides the only data source, models constructed from *different participants'* recollections may prove useful. If participants order complex, ambiguous decision processes in their recollections, then different participants may focus on different parts of the process and develop different models of it. Therefore, if several researchers each developed a model of a particular decision process based on one participant's recollections, discussions of the subsequent differences in models might improve the researchers' understanding of the process. Jick (1979) discusses this as one of the benefits of examining different organizational members' views of the same phenomenon.

The suggestions just offered may not lead to a complete resolution of the problems posed by the fact that different data sources produce different decision models. However, they may help to minimize the biasing effects of primary reliance on a single data source and to reconcile some of the differences between decision process models based on different data sources. Systematic research using multiple data sources may also help identify and improve our understanding of the factors accounting for these differences.

Once the basic questions about the nature of the strategic decision process have been answered, it will be appropriate to address these questions:

Do strategic planning systems make the strategic decision process more comprehensive? Do they make the process more effective?

How do structural factors such as complexity, centralization, and formalization affect the strategic decision process?

How do strategic decision processes differ in periods of revolutionary change as compared to periods of equilibrium?

4

The Political Perspective

I n this chapter, I will discuss a number of themes developed by
strategic management researchers under the general heading of
power and political processes in strategic management. Much of
this work has its intellectual roots in the disciplines of political science, social psychology, anthropology, and sociology and is consistent with Allison's Model III or bureaucratic politics paradigm. This
chapter deals with political processes as distinct from organizational processes, which were the subject of the previous chapter.

Whether the political and organizational approach to the study
of strategic management is appropriate depends on the assumptions
made about superordinate goals. If we view strategic management
as an intendedly rational attempt to achieve superordinate goals,
the study or organizational and cognitive processes may explain the
constraints on an organization's rationality and its departures from
rationality in its strategic planning. If, on the other hand, we assume
that strategic decisions are not plans for rationally achieving superordinate goals, but are the result of bargaining among individuals
attempting to achieve their own personal goals (Abell, 1975), then
the study of political processes becomes appropriate.

Allison (1971, pp. 163–84) discusses the basic characteristics of
the bureaucratic or government politics paradigm. In this paradigm,
organizational decisions and actions are the result of political processes, bargaining processes, and power games within organizations. Organizations are composed of players in positions who en-
gage in games to enhance their own power and prestige.

As was mentioned in chapter 1, my discussion of the political perspective on strategic management has been influenced by Allison's discussion of the bureaucratic politics model. Other works in political science have also been very useful in understanding intraorganizational political processes. Two that are very often cited are Neustadt's *Presidential Power* (1960) and Crozier's *The Bureaucratic Phenomenon* (1964). A reader by Rourke (1965) entitled *Bureaucratic Power in National Politics* contains a number of articles providing background on the political science contribution to the understanding of the politics of the strategic decision process. Prominent political scientists, including Philip Selznick, Herbert Simon, and Graham Allison, discuss the effects of constituencies on administrative agencies' decision making, the power of bureaucratic expertise, the struggle for power that constitutes bureaucratic politics, and public control of bureaucracy.

I will begin this chapter with a treatment of external sources of power and influence on strategies. Next, I will discuss the sources of power within organizations. I will then discuss the ways in which power relationships become formalized and legitimated. Here, I will cover the topics of organizational ideology and culture. Finally, I will discuss the exercise of power and political maneuvering in strategic decision making. Figure 4–1 shows how these topics are related. The relationship between these topics will be discussed later in the chapter.

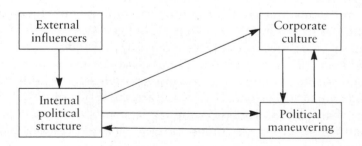

Figure 4–1. *Relationship between the Elements of the Political Perspective on Strategic Decision Making*

External Environmental Influence on Strategic Decision Making

Henry Mintzberg, in his book *Power In and Around Organizations* (1983), has provided a clearly organized summary list of the individuals, groups, and organizations that may influence the strategic management of organizations. He has categorized these into four broad groups: *owners* of the organization, *associates* who deal with it, associations that represent *employers*, and the various *publics* that surround the organization.

According to Mintzberg, ownership of organizations can be either concentrated or dispersed (as in the case of a company owned by a small number of institutions versus one owned by a large number of individuals), and the owners may be deeply involved in operations or relatively detached. When ownership is concentrated and owners are involved, they have greater power over decision making.

Common associates for a particular business may include suppliers, clients, partners, and competitors. Often, organizations in these categories do not become part of the power system. However, they become powerful to the extent that they provide essential inputs to the organization.

Employee associations are the means by which employees, usually part of the internal coalition of an organization, exert external pressure. These include unions of various kinds and professional societies.

An organization's publics are technically the most detached from the organization. They fall into three categories. The first category includes the surveyors of the public interest (such as newspaper editorialists, priests, and teachers). The second category involves various forms of government, while the third includes special interest groups (Mintzberg, 1983, pp. 32–46).

Those who seek to influence strategy often form coalitions. Mintzberg has divided external coalitions into three basic types: dominated, divided, and passive. The *dominated* external coalition develops when one influencer or a subset of influencers acts in concert to dominate the others. This allows for the dominant influencer(s) to essentially control strategic decision. In the *divided* coalition, power is divided among independent influencers so that the organization must respond to conflicting demands. This obviously creates potential for conflict and political maneuvering. Finally, Mintzberg uses the term *passive* external coalition to refer to the situation where there are numerous influencers and the power of each one is small. In this situation, management has broad power and discretion in adapting to general goals.

Other strategic management researchers use the term *stakeholder* to refer to those who try to change the organization to accommodate their desires. Freeman defines a stakeholder as "any group or individual who can affect or is affected by the achievement of the organization's objectives" (1984, p. 46). Common stakeholders include stockholders, suppliers, unions, government agencies, consumer groups, and trade associations. Stakeholders have various types of power bases including formal or voting power, economic power, and political power (Freeman, 1984, pp. 60–64).

Sociologists and political scientists have dealt with the factors that give power to external influencers. Thompson (1967, pp. 19–38) describes what he calls the "pluralism of task environments," the fact that there are multiple groups or individuals in any organization's environment that may have an impact on the organization's goals, strategy, and behavior. Thompson, drawing on the work of Emerson (1962), says that the extent to which an organization is dependent on some element of its environment depends on the organization's need for resources or performances that the particular element can provide and the ability of other elements to provide the same resources or performance. Thus, a manufacturing firm is dependent on a financial organization to the extent that the firm needs financial resources and financial resources are not available from other sources. The hospital is dependent on physicians in the community to the extent that the hospital needs patients and that physicians monopolize the capacity to refer patients to hospitals (Thompson, 1967, p. 30).

These ideas have their roots in sociological concepts such as "legitimacy" (Parsons, 1960). Parsons suggests that society must grant an organization legitimacy in order for it to survive. Pfeffer and Salancik (1978, pp. 24–27) suggest that organizations attempt to act in such a way that they ensure their legitimacy in the view of the organizations on which they are dependent for vital resources. However, this becomes extremely difficult when these organizations have different demands and different criteria for assessing legitimacy. A study by Pickle and Friedlander (1967) shows that different potential interest groups may in fact have different criteria for evaluating the legitimacy of an organization's behavior. Their results show very low correlations between executives' perceptions of the satisfaction of various stakeholders and their organizations' performance (Pickle and Friedlander, 1967, p. 171).

Eric Rhenman (1973) notes the importance of the work of sociologists such as Philip Selznick (1949) in understanding the formation of organizational goals in response to the external environment. Rhenman suggests that these principles are important in determining the proper approach to long-range planning in a particular organization. Mazzolini (1979) discusses the types of influence governments have on the strategies of government-controlled firms.

Murray (1978) presents evidence from a study of a major electric utility that shows that plans of strategic significance are "negotiated" with external parties or influences, often in a kind of incremental way (1978, p. 968). Murray found that initial strategy and supporting plans were intendedly rational, but that external pressure groups forced numerous incremental revisions as the strategy was being implemented. In this study, the power of the management of the company was quite small in comparison to the power of other institutions in the firm's environment. Also, the decision was quite *fragmented* in that the approval of many groups was needed. These factors contributed to the incremental, negotiated character of the decision.

Dirsmith and Covaleski (1983) have pointed out that Murray's study shows that "organizations both influence and are influenced by the environment through the exchange of information" (p. 139). They also assert that this mutual influence or dialectic process leads to negotiation between the organization and its external influencers about appropriate standards for measuring performance (1983, p. 146).

In summary, firms face pressures from a variety of external influencers or stakeholders. The pressures are more or less intense depending on the power of these external influencers and the co-ordination among them. I have discussed a number of common influencers and demonstrated that there may be conflicts among their demands. Organizations will comply with demands of various stakeholder groups to the extent that they are *dependent* on these groups. I have discussed some of the work in political science and sociology that provides a foundation for the study of external influence on strategic decision making. In the next section of this chapter, I will discuss the ways external influence is reflected in *internal* political structures.

Internal Political Structures

What determines the distribution of power *within* decision-making groups in companies? Researchers have generally found that control of critical resources or ability to resolve strategic uncertainties is a source of individual power in organizations (Pfeffer, 1981, pp. 101–115). Crozier (1964) was one of the first to demonstrate this in his pioneering study of a French industrial monopoly. In this organization, he found evidence of a great deal of intraorganizational conflict and concluded that the struggle for power was at the root of these conflicts (1964, p. 139). He cited Talcott Parsons (1960) in developing his assertion that power and its effects on the decision process must become the central concern of organizational theory (1964, pp. 145–50).

Crozier discussed the relative power and the bases of power of four groups within the monopoly: production workers, maintenance workers, lower supervisors, and the management team. He found that the power of the management team was severely limited by the rationalization of the work process, an observation echoed later by Kanter (1977). Somewhat surprisingly, Crozier found that the maintenance workers had a good deal of power in such a system because machine breakdown was "the last source of uncertainty remaining in a completely routinized organizational system" (1964,

p. 154). The secret of the power of the maintenance workers in this system was that they were able to control maintenance information themselves and restrict access to it by others in the organization. Control of various types of information is a frequently mentioned basis of power in later studies following Crozier's work.

Hickson, Hinings, Lee, Schneck, and Pennings (1971) extended Crozier's work through their suggestion that the power of individuals or subunits in an organization is based on their ability to deal with areas of problematic uncertainty for the organization. In a study of breweries, they found that the power of a subunit was related to its ability to reduce the unpredictability of the future for other units, the extent to which its work could be performed by other units, and its centrality in the work flow. All these factors allow the subunit to manage uncertainty for other units.

Jemison (1981a) explained the comparative impacts of internal (organizational) and external (environmental) sources of influence on strategic decisions. He pointed out that many earlier studies on power in organizations have focused on one of these sources of influence to the exclusion of the others. In his study, a questionnaire was administered to 124 senior executives in fifteen organizations. The results supported the conclusion that environmentally related activities are more important in explaining influence in strategic decisions than are internal organizational activities. This suggests that departments dealing with the environment have more influence on strategic decisions (Jemison, 1981a, p. 86).

Spekman (1979) found that information that helped resolve uncertainty was a source of power in organizational decision making. His study focused on the role of the boundary spanner—the person at the interface between the organization and its environment. Spekman found that the perceived power of boundary spanners is greater when the organization faces a high level of environmental uncertainty. Jemison (1984) found that boundary spanners have a great deal of influence on strategic decisions and that the relative influence of different boundary-spanning roles is related to an organization's technology.

In an ethnographic study of a large corporation, Kanter illustrates a number of ideas about organizational power and intracompany politics found in the works of sociologists such as C. Wright Mills, Michael Crozier, and Robert Merton (Kanter, 1977, pp. 164–206). She notes that political processes are necessary for large bureaucratic organizations to operate effectively and discusses the types of power relationships produced by the division of labor and subsequent interdependence of organizational members and the decentralization of organizational structure.

Mintzberg (1983, p. 115) provides one of the most thorough and complete descriptions of internal political structures in organizations. He begins with a discussion of the five basic groups of internal influencers. The *operators* are those who take the actions that produce the basic outputs of the organization. The CEO delegates to the *line managers* formal responsibility for the decisions and actions affecting the operators. The *analysts* are concerned with designing and running formal systems to achieve coordination as well as providing advice on those systems. Planners, production schedulers, and accountants are examples of analysts. The *support staff* provides advice on certain specialized decisions and has responsibility for various support functions. The support staff includes those people working in such places as the cafeteria, mail room, and public relations department.

He then discusses the power bases of each of these internal influencers and uses this discussion to develop four basic influence systems. The first is based on authority, the second on ideology, the third on expertise, and the fourth on politics. These influence systems are unifying forces for the internal coalition.

The system of authority is based on formal power vested in the positions of the organization. The CEO establishes this system by delegating authority to others in the organization and by designing the organization's superstructure, establishing the system of rewards, and utilizing this system and others to control behavior. The second influence system, the system of ideology, rests on a set of "beliefs about the organization, shared by its members, that distinguishes [the organization] from other organizations" (1983, p. 152). The third influence system rests on the power of expertise. Expertise creates an informal system that, to some extent, replaces the system of authority. Mintzberg draws on the work of Gouldner, Kanter, Crozier, Hickson, and Pfeffer and Salancik to support the assertion that power in an organization is bestowed on those who find a critical function in which to practice their irreplaceable expertise (1983, p. 170). The final influence system is based on the political processes that emerge as a result of the fact that delegation of authority gives discretion to lower-level members of the organization. According to Mintzberg, this discretion is used to serve the parochial interests of those who possess it (1983, p. 179).

Different types of internal coalitions are based on each of these influence systems. Mintzberg identifies the five types of internal coalitions: personalized, bureaucratic, ideologic, professional, and politicized (1983, 234–42).

There are fifteen possible combinations between the three types of external coalitions and the five types of internal coalitions. However, Mintzberg singles out six as being the most likely to occur in the real world. He calls these six "power configurations" and has named them the Instrument, the Closed System, the Autocracy, the Missionary, the Meritocracy, and the Political Arena.

The Instrument is a power configuration in which the organization serves a dominant external influencer. As its name implies, such a power configuration is an instrument for achieving the ends of the dominant coalition. Political game-playing is at a minimum. The Closed System involves a passive external coalition and a bureaucratic structure permitting those at the top of the organization to gain the power. Survival is one of the most important goals and there is some room for politics.

In the Autocracy, a strong dynamic leader dominates the organization, which in turn faces a passive external coalition. Goals reflect the leader's preference to a great extent. A Missionary organization is dominated by ideology, which tends to render the external coalition passive. Ideology provides the organization's goals, on which there is usually strong agreement.

The Meritocracy is based on expertise. However, the presence of conflicting experts creates the possibility of political behavior. Finally, the Political Arena, as its name implies, is characterized by conflict in the external coalition and political power struggles within the organization (Mintzberg, 1983, pp. 312–14).

Mintzberg (1984) has discussed the changes in power configurations over time as the organization moves through different stages in its life cycle. He suggested that organizations in the stage of formation are generally autocracies. Those in the development stage generally conform to the instrument or missionary power configuration. Mature organizations are generally meritocracies or closed systems. Declining organizations tend to become political arenas (1984, p. 213).

Hirschman, in his classic book, *Exit, Voice, and Loyalty* (1970), discusses the three options available to organizational members who are dissatisfied with the organization's performance or behavior. They may either choose to leave (exit), make their dissatisfactions known and attempt to change the organization (voice), or remain supportive of the organization without voicing disagreements (loyalty). In business organizations, those members with the ability to resolve critical uncertainties are likely to be able to use voice more effectively than those without such ability. The members who do not control critical uncertainties may find they must choose between exit and loyalty, neither of which can be expected to have much impact on the organization.

In summary, the power to influence strategic decisions within a company comes from the ability to resolve uncertainty and to control critical external contingencies. Power manifests itself in different configurations depending on the external coalitions facing a firm and the coalitions within it. These configurations change as the organization evolves.

Organizational Culture and Ideology: Legitimation and Solidification of Political Processes

Pfeffer (1981) suggests that power distributions become institutionalized in organizational culture, which can be defined in terms of shared meanings and beliefs (1981, pp. 298–303). Therefore, the study of corporate culture may help us understand the internal political structure of organizations. Further, the study of culture provides insights into the *processes* by which power may shape the perceptions of organizational members through stories, ideologies, and rituals. Corporate cultures have recently been the subject of great popular interest. A best-selling book by Deal and Kennedy

(1982) discusses a number of topics commonly included under the heading of culture, including corporate values, heroes, rites, and rituals.

The book *In Search of Excellence* attests to the influence of corporate culture on top-level strategic decision making and organizational performance (Peters and Waterman, 1982, pp. 74–76). According to Peters and Waterman, strong cultures were an essential characteristic of the excellent companies they studied. Poorer-performing companies also had strong cultures. However, these were dysfunctional and focused internally rather than toward customers.

Pettigrew (1979) defines the term *culture* as an "amalgam of beliefs, ideology, language, ritual, and myth" (1979, p. 572). He suggests that leaders may create cultures that promote commitment through the use of these elements. In his review, Pettigrew cites a number of anthropologists and sociologists from whom the concepts underlying the study of culture come. He also advocates the use of longitudinal field research for the study of culture.

Schall (1983) discusses the use of communication patterns in organizations as means of defining an organization's culture. This theme is also dealt with by Broms and Gahmberg (1983) and Barley (1983), who suggest the study of signs and symbols as a means of understanding an organization's culture.

The concept of ideology is closely related to culture. Starbuck says, "Ideologies are logically integrated clusters of beliefs, values, rituals, and symbols," and that interactions between ideologies are controlled by ceremonies and rituals (1982, p. 1). In general, however, the term *ideology* has a somewhat different meaning than *culture*; in some ways, it is more restricted and, in some ways, broader. Ideology is generally taken to mean the cognitive or belief aspect of culture. Ideology can be shared by a group of organizations, though *culture* is generally used with respect to a single company.

Dunbar, Dutton, and Torbert (1982) address the dilemma involved in attempting to develop ideologies that simultaneously promote stability and change. Through a case study, they illustrate ways of thwarting change attempts that violate a strongly held organizational ideology.

Brunsson (1982) notes another type of dilemma created by organizational ideology. Much effort has been spent developing techniques and approaches designed to improve the rationality of organizational decision making. However, Brunsson notes that some irrationalities may be necessary requirements for organizational actions. Choices are facilitated by narrow and clear organizational ideologies, and actions are facilitated by irrational decision-making procedures that maximize motivation and commitment.

Meyer (1982), through structured observation of nineteen hospitals, finds support for the assertion that harmonious organizational ideologies tend to be found in organizations with simple structures, while discordant ideologies are found more often in companies with elaborate structures.

Organizational stories and myths are the most important means by which culture is communicated to organizational members. Such stories also provide guidance for making strategic decisions consistent with the culture. Selznick states that such stories are "efforts to state, in the language of uplift and idealism, what is distinctive about the aims and methods of the enterprise" (1957, p. 151). Organizational myths and stories, as means of communicating and maintaining culture, have received a good deal of attention from academics (Dandridge, Mitroff, and Joyce, 1980).

Organizational stories may be the best source of data on organizational culture. Martin, Feldman, Hatch, and Sitkin (1983) examined published institutional stories and identified common themes in stories told by employees in a wide variety of organizations. These themes include: Who breaks the rules? Is the big boss human? Can a little person rise to the top? Will I get fired? How will the organization deal with obstacles? Martin et al. claim that stories deal with common dualities in organizational life, including equality versus inequality, security versus insecurity, and control versus lack of control. The authors note that such stories also provide self-serving rationalization of the past and suggest patterns of responsibility for good and bad outcomes.

What then is the link between culture, strategic decision processes, and political structures in companies? Riley (1983) links the concepts of power and political processes to the concept of culture. She suggests that political maneuverings *create* culture and that culture serves to legitimate certain types of political behavior and to define correct behavior.

The relevance of culture to strategic decision making is clear. Culture serves to specify what is and is not acceptable in an organization. Therefore, culture will affect the types of strategic alternatives that are seriously considered for dealing with a particular strategic problem and which criteria will be used in evaluating these alternatives. Culture will also affect the patterns of political maneuvering that may occur in organizations. The topic of political maneuvering will be discussed next.

Political Maneuvering: The Exercise of Power in Strategic Decision Making

Some researchers have studied the specific ways power and political processes affect the strategy formulation process. Narayanan and Fahey (1982) discuss the ways coalitions form around strategic issues and how power operates at the various stages of the decision process. They develop a political model of the strategic decision-making process that contains five stages. These include activation (when individuals become aware of strategic issues), mobilization (where issue awareness is elevated from the individual to the organizational level), coalescence (in which a coalition forms within the organization to sponsor a desired solution to the strategic problem or a set of alternatives), encounter (in which the coalition confronts others in the organization in an attempt to sell its solution), and decision (in which zones of consensus and dissent become more clear and are dealt with in some manner prior to reaching a decision) (pp. 28–31).

In the middle three stages, there is ample opportunity for the exercise of power. Narayanan and Fahey note that since information is exchanged during mobilization, those who control information can strongly influence the decision at this stage. During their discussion of the coalescence stage, they cite MacMillan (1978), who points out that unequal power of coalition members leads to the emergence of a political structure within the coalition (p. 29).

In the process of negotiation during the encounter stage, there are *gambits,* which are strategies used by a coalition to achieve its ends (p. 30).

MacMillan and Jones (1986) also deal with coalition formation in strategic decision making (pp. 60–70), the ways in which political structures evolve in organizations, and the effects these have on political strategy formulation (pp. 64–70). This provides the basis for their discussion of stakeholder analysis and the use of political tools to influence decision outcomes.

Kanter (1977) discusses some of the more common techniques for obtaining power, including the cultivation of visibility and the use of alliances. Mintzberg also addresses a number of political games that can be used to achieve political ends.

Farrel and Peterson (1982) consider patterns of individual political behavior in organizations. They develop a useful typology of political behavior based on three dimensions: internal/external, vertical/lateral, and legitimate/illegitimate. Internal political action or influence attempts involve only those within the organization, while external action involves attempting to gain influence through contacts outside the organization. Vertical political behavior involves contact with those at levels other than one's own in the chain of command, while lateral influence attempts involve those at one's own level. Finally, political behavior may take forms sanctioned by the organization (legitimate) or it may take unsanctioned forms (illegitimate).

Conclusion

In this chapter, I have shown that external forces, rather than cognitive or organizational processes, can be viewed as the major constraint on strategic decision making. In fact, strategy formulation can be studied as an attempt to respond to to conflicting demands from external groups, each having a different base of power.

Those who view strategic decisions as responses to external pressures would adopt different explanations for decisions than those who focus on cognitive or organizational factors. They would focus on the characteristics and power of external influencers, assuming that these are the major determinants of decision outcomes. Future research should focus on the identification of the most important external influencers in different industries and their bases of power within the basic resource-dependence perspective.

Power and internal political processes within an organization reflect these external pressures, with the greatest amount of power being held by those who can effectively manage external influencers upon whom the organization is dependent. Corporate cultures, in turn, reflect the political processes and power configurations within organizations and help to solidify them. Corporate culture and the internal political structure affect the process of political maneuvering. The outcomes of this process, in turn, affect future political structure and culture. These points are summarized in figure 4–1.

In general it is difficult to offer recommendations for managing political processes grounded in controlled, multicase empirical research. Thus far, there has been a great deal of conceptual work based on some field observations, but comparatively little research designed to test the assertions found in conceptual pieces. It is hoped that future reviews on this topic will deal more with recommendations firmly grounded in empirical research.

A number of interesting research questions have yet to be answered within the basic political perspective. Some of these are:

What are the critical uncertainties and, hence, the specific sources of power in different industries?

What are the company and industry characteristics that determine the sorts of political games that will be most effective in influencing strategic decision outcomes?

What are the most common stimuli that lead to changes in corporate cultures (and, hence, internal political structures)?

What are the environmental, industry, and company factors that determine whether major changes in corporate culture will be successful?

The research reviewed in this chapter deals with the sources of power and its use in strategic decision making. Therefore, it is consistent with the Model III view, which suggests that strategic decisions are the result of political influence in bargaining processes. The research I have reviewed provides insights into the operation of political processes.

This chapter concludes the summaries of the three major perspectives for explaining strategic decision outcomes. As I said in chapter 1, different explanations for decision outcomes produce different prescriptions for improving future decisions. Combining the perspectives allows us to make intelligent use of multiple prescriptions. In the next chapter, I will discuss the implications of each perspective for the development of strategic decision aids and the prescriptions consistent with each perspective. I will then discuss a way of combining the three perspectives in theory. This discussion will be followed by a description of a method of structured conflict by which multiple prescriptions may be integrated.

5
Three Types of Prescriptions for Improving Strategic Decision Making

In previous chapters, I have dealt with the *explanation* of strategic decisions. This material can help us understand the differences between recommendations for improving strategic decisions. The reflective management practitioner faces a difficult task in evaluating such recommendations. The proliferation of strategic decision aids in the past few decades is documented in several reviews (Grant and King, 1982; Mitroff and Mason, 1982). Further, the diversity of recommendations can be bewildering. On the one hand, there are analytical recommendations based on highly structured approaches to planning such as the Boston Consulting Group matrix with its cash cows, stars, question marks, and dogs. On the other hand, there are recommendations from sources such as Quinn's *Strategies for Change* (1980) and Peters and Waterman's *In Search of Excellence* (1982) that focus on improving corporate culture and employee motivation and minimize the importance of finding the "analytically correct" solution to strategic problems. It is not simply that the latter recommendations concentrate on implementation while the former concentrate on formulation. Quinn as well as Peters and Waterman suggest a different approach

Some of the material in this chapter is reprinted with permission from Charles R. Schwenk, "Three Perspectives on Improving Strategic Decisions," *Long Range Planning* 1987, 20, Pergamon Journals Ltd.

to formulation that is influenced by the demands and needs of those involved in implementation and that is not dominated by formal or structured approaches.

Given the diversity of recommendations, how does one choose among them or combine them intelligently? This chapter attempts to clarify the basic differences between the recommendations so that they can be used more effectively. In order to understand the differences between prescriptions for improving strategy, it is necessary to understand the ways decision outcomes are commonly explained. Therefore, the material in the three previous chapters forms the basis for the discussion in this chapter.

In the next sections of this chapter, recommendations for improving strategic decisions will be classified into the three categories corresponding to Allison's three basic approaches. The recommendations discussed do not constitute an exhaustive list of all those available in the literature. However, they provide good examples of recommendations from the three perspectives. Examples from each category will be discussed in detail. In the concluding section, a model that integrates the cognitive organizational and political perspectives will be developed and recommendations will be offered for using multiple perspectives in strategic decision making.

As was stated earlier, Allison showed that decisions can be explained as an intendedly rational choice of the whole organization (model I: unitary rational actor), as the product of organizational processes (model II: organizational processes), or as the result of political bargaining and compromise (model III: bureaucratic politics). According to Allison, these perspectives represent the largely implicit conceptual models that analysts use to explain decision outcomes. Through Allison's three models, we can understand the three basic types of recommendations for improving strategic decisions.

If decisions are viewed from a model I perspective, cognitive processes of key decisionmakers become important. Improving these decisionmakers' understanding of strategic problems and their cognitive processes become the main goals of a strategic decision aid. Many existing strategic decision aids are focused on cognitive processes. However, as Allison points out, organizational processes and political bargaining processes may also affect the outcomes of strategic decisions.

If decisions are viewed as the outcomes of organizational processes, it follows that decision aids should improve the organizational processes through which decisions are reached. Recommendations consistent with model II generally focus on increasing the thoroughness of data analysis and the comprehensiveness of each stage of the decision process. It is assumed that comprehensiveness will improve decision quality.

Those who feel power and political processes determine decision outcomes claim that political criteria must be used in evaluating decision quality. Freeman, for example, suggests that high-quality decisions are those that satisfy the desires of stakeholders who have power to affect implementation of a strategic decision (Freeman, 1984, pp. 24–27). Quinn says that high-quality decisions are those that produce consensus and commitment (Quinn, 1980, p. 27). Normative recommendations consistent with this model are intended to improve the representation of critical stakeholders and increase the changes of consensus. Table 5–1 summarizes the normative prescriptions for improving strategic decision making that are consistent with each of the three models.

This categorization is not meant to imply that each prescription is grounded in *only* one model of the decision process. Most have implications for two or more of the models. However, each approach is *primarily* concerned with *either* cognitive, organizational, *or* political processes.

Normative Prescriptions from the Rational-Choice Perspective

Prescriptions consistent with the traditional perspective are de-signed to help managers identify the most important contingencies to be considered in rational decision making. These prescriptions

Table 5–1
Three Categories of Normative Prescriptions

Model	Goal	Sources of Normative Prescriptions
Model I: rational-choice and cognitive processes	Improve problem comprehension by providing frameworks	BCG Matrix (Henderson, 1979) STRATPORT (Larreche and Srinivasan, 1981) CP/IA Matrix (Hofer and Schendel, 1978, p. 71–81) PIMS (Abell and Hammond, 1977) Market Life Cycles (Hofer and Schendel, 1978) Industry Analysis (Porter, 1980)
	Improve problem comprehension by clarifying decisionmakers' own frameworks	Multiple Scenarios (Linneman and Klein, 1983) Decision Analysis (Thomas and Schwenk, 1983) SPIRE (Klein and Newman, 1980) Influence Diagrams (Diffenbach, 1982) Cognitive Mapping (Axelrod, 1976; Eden et al., 1979)
Model II: organizational processes	Increase the quality of scanning and formulation processes	Formal Planning Systems (Lorange and Vancil, 1977; Naylor, 1979; Steiner, 1979) Regular, Irregular, and Continuous Scanning (Fahey and King, 1977) GLOBESCAN (Hofer and Haller, 1980) QUEST (Hanus, 1982) LEAP (Preble, 1982) Structural Prescriptions (Chandler, 1962; Galbraith and Kazanjian, 1986; Williamson, 1975; Burgelman and Sayles, 1986)
Model III: political processes	Improve stakeholder representation and management	Dependence Reduction/Autonomy Strategies (Pfeffer and Salancik, 1978; Sexty, 1980) Stakeholder Management (Freeman, 1984) Strategic Assumptions Analysis (Mason and Mitroff, 1981) Integrating social responsibility into Planning (Carroll and Hoy, 1984) Logical Incrementalism (Quinn, 1980) Social Response Matrix (Channon, 1979) Intensity Diffusion/Convergence Analysis (Wilson, 1974) Cultural Risk Matrix (Schwartz and Davis, 1981)

are based on different types of contingencies including market share, stage in the product life cycle, and competitive dynamics of an industry.

Probably the best known of these types of aids is the Boston Consulting Group's Product Portfolio (Henderson, 1979; Abell and Hammond, 1979; McNamee, 1985). This approach is based on the assumption that market share and market growth rates are the most important factors to consider in developing strategy for a multi-business company. Each of a company's products are plotted on the market growth and market share dimensions. Larreche and Srinivasan (1981) have designed a decision support system to assist top managers and corporate planners in formulating strategies within the context of the product portfolio.

The basic product portfolio makes some very restrictive assumptions and has been criticized for this reason. Researchers have pointed out that the assumptions about the importance of market share and market growth may be inaccurate and that these assumptions lead to questionable recommendations for products in various categories, particularly the "dog" category (Woo, 1984).

Because of these criticisms, other matrices have been developed that are based on less restrictive assumptions. One of the best known of these is the competitive position/industry attractiveness (CP/IA) matrix (Abell and Hammond, 1979; Hofer and Schendel, 1978). In this matrix, the dimensions of competitive position and industry attractiveness are defined by multiple criteria that are weighted according to their importance. In the CP/IA matrix, management judgment is used to define and weight the criteria. Once products or product lines are positioned in the matrix, strategies can be developed for each.

Another type of portfolio matrix has been suggested by Hofer and Schendel (1978, pp. 102–4, 182–84). This portfolio is based on two dimensions: the product life cycle and a company's competitive position, both of which are determined by management judgment.

A data base exists that can supplement management judgment in defining and weighting the criteria that contribute to competitive position and industry attractiveness. This is the PIMS data base (Abell and Hammond, 1979; McNamee, 1985) containing information on industry- and business-level variables provided by over 150 companies on over 1,500 lines of business. This data can be used to identify industry- and business-level factors that are most closely related to various measures of profitability. These can be examined as the most promising competitive-position and industry-attractiveness criteria.

One of the most popular recent approaches to formulating strategy at the business level is provided by Porter (1980). His specification of the five major competitive forces in an industry provides the basis for recommendations for competing in an industry. These competitive forces included threat of entry, threat of substitutes, power of buyers, power of suppliers, and level of rivalry.

Some decision aids are intended not to provide a ready-made conceptual framework, but to clarify decisionmakers' own understanding of strategic problems. One of the best-known techniques for improving understanding of strategic problems involves the use of multiple scenarios. A scenario is basically a narrative about the future. Multiple scenarios provide conflicting narratives to decisionmakers. Klein and Linneman (1981) describe a variety of different approaches to scenario generation and use. All of these involve certain key activities. Assumptions about the environment and the company that seem realistic are identified; these are then modified to create optimistic and pessimistic assumption sets; these alternative sets of assumptions are then used to create alternative scenarios for use by management. As Klein and Linneman point out, there is a great deal of variance among companies in the number of scenarios used, the formality of the process used to develop them, their time horizon, and the ways they are used in planning. However, in all cases, they are used to clarify alternative views of a company's future in order to improve decisionmakers' understanding of the strategies that might be required to deal with the future (Klein and Linneman, 1981; Linneman and Klein, 1983). Decision analysis has been recommended as a method that helps strategic decisionmakers understand the risks and returns associated with various courses of action (Schwenk and Thomas, 1983). It might therefore be helpful in the development of multiple scenarios.

The Systematic Procedure for Identifying Relevant Environments (SPIRE) technique is designed to help decisionmakers clarify their views on the relevant environments for strategic planning (Klein and Newman, 1980). In this procedure, decisionmakers identify the most important parts of their organization, the most important environmental factors, and the ways these might impact the organization. This information provides the basis of the construction of a diagram indicating the impacts of environmental factors on the organization's "strategic components." Influence diagramming is a related technique that provides a graphic representation of strategists' beliefs about the factors that impact on a particular strategic issue (Diffenbach, 1982). Influence diagramming makes the interrelationships between these factors visible and explicit.

These approaches are similar to what has been called cognitive mapping (Eden, Jones, and Sims, 1979; Axelrod, 1976). Cognitive maps consist of concepts about aspects of the decision environment and beliefs about cause-and-effect relationships between them. Such maps serve as interpretive lenses that help decisionmakers select certain aspects of an issue as important for diagnosis. Axelrod has developed methods for representing cognitive maps diagrammatically. Though they are often used to represent individual world views, they may be used to represent shared assumptions among a group of strategic decisionmakers, which makes them useful in the study of strategic problem formulation. Axelrod notes that the purpose of cognitive mapping is not to represent a person's entire belief system. Rather, he says, "A cognitive map is designed to capture the structure of the causal assertions of a person with respect to a particular policy domain, and generate the consequences that follow from this structure" (1976, p. 58).

Of course, many of these approaches for improving understanding may also be seen as approaches to increasing information or even for improving organizational processes. However, they all deal primarily with the improvement of cognitive processes in strategic decisions.

The personal computer may make the use of these types of decision aids easier and more rewarding. McNamee (1985) has described computer programs for use in connection with experience curve analysis, portfolio analysis, and multiple scenario analysis.

Normative Prescriptions Involving Organizational Processes

The normative prescriptions in this section are designed to improve the comprehensiveness of information gathering and the systems through which strategies are formulated and implemented. Many provide step-by-step instructions for information gathering and strategy formulation.

For example, George Steiner (1979) provides a model of the strategic planning process that includes a step-by-step description of the activities that should be undertaken as part of formal planning. These activities include an assessment of the major internal and external pressures and an analysis of the organization's data base as part of the situation audit, followed by strategy formulation and medium- and short-range planning and programming.

Steiner's recommendations focus on improving the comprehensiveness and quality of each of the steps in the process. It is felt that this will improve the overall quality of a strategic decision. Prescriptions for the design and improvement of formal planning systems abound (Lorange and Vancil, 1977; Naylor, 1979). Since each of these sources contains excellent summaries of these prescriptions, they will not be reviewed here.

Steiner and others have recommended at least three types of strategic planning systems, each appropriate for a different type of organization and environment. These are the top-down, bottom-up, and combination approaches (Steiner, 1979, pp. 63–64). In the top-down approach, those executives at the top of the company are responsible for formulating companywide strategy. In the bottom-up approach, those at the divisional level have the responsibility for formulating divisional strategies which are then integrated at the corporate level. In the combination approach, strategies are formulated and refined at both the corporate and divisional levels in an iterative process.

Techniques also exist for improving the comprehensiveness or quality of information gathering and use in environmental analysis. Environmental scanning systems include irregular, regular, and continuous scanning systems (Fahey and King, 1977). Irregular scanning systems are used to identify the implications of a major environmental change that has already occurred. In these systems, as the name implies, scanning occurs at irregular intervals, as the need arises. Regular scanning systems are used to provide information for regularly recurring organizational decisions. Scanning is done at regular intervals and is coordinated with the recurring decisions. Finally, continuous scanning systems involve the continuous monitoring of the environment to identify information that might be relevant for a wide range of strategic and operational decisions.

Techniques are also available for scanning specific environments. For example, Hofer and Haller's (1980) GLOBESCAN is useful in scanning the international environment to identify potential areas for foreign investment. GLOBESCAN involves systematic procedures for identifying the risks and rewards associated with international ventures in particular foreign countries and developing strategies for managing these ventures.

In addition to these basic scanning approaches, there are more specific techniques for the development of forecasts. These techniques include QUEST, a quick environmental scanning technique (Hanus, 1982), and LEAP, a forecasting technique that uses expert opinion to develop consensus forecasts in a manner similar to the Delphi technique (Preble, 1982).

The final set of prescriptions to be discussed in this section deals with the use of structural change to improve strategic decision making and organizational performance. Since Chandler's classic work *Strategy and Structure* (1962), researchers have suggested that the divisional structure is most appropriate for companies with a diverse range of products or businesses (Galbraith and Kazanjian, 1986). In the divisional structure, each business is represented by a separate division that has a degree of autonomy in the development of its own overall strategy. Williamson (1975, p. 137) has praised the "M-Form" organizational structure, which he describes as a divisional structure with appropriate coordination from the corporate level to ensure that all divisions contribute to the overall strategy and that synergy is achieved.

Burgelman and Sayles (1986) have discussed the importance of encouraging innovation and internal development of new ventures within companies. They suggest that structural changes can be used to promote the development of innovative new ventures. Management must first assess proposals for internal entrepreneurial ventures in terms of their strategic importance to the firm and the extent to which they are related to existing operations.

They then recommend a set of nine design alternatives representing a continuum on the dimensions of strategic importance and operational relatedness. At one end of the continuum, for ventures with high strategic importance and operational relatedness, they recommend "direct integration" in which the venture is administratively and operationally integrated into the mainstream of the business. At the other end, they recommend "complete spin-off" for ventures with low strategic importance and operational relatedness. Here, the individual internal entrepreneur is allowed to start his or her own business with few if any links to the parent corporation (Burgelman and Sayles, 1986, pp. 179–88).

These prescriptions for the design and change of organizational processes and structures could, of course, affect the cognitive processes of organizational members and the political realities within the organization. However, since they deal *primarily* with organizational factors, they are included in this section.

Normative Prescriptions Involving Political Processes

Many examples discussed in the first chapter of this book show the failure of a technically sound strategy that did not meet stakeholders' needs. Because of failures such as this, there is increased interest in techniques for managing stakeholders and political processes. As was mentioned earlier, stakeholders are the individuals or groups who have a *stake* in the outcome of a strategic decision and who have some power to affect its implementation.

Knowing that organizations are subject to external political pressures and that political processes pervade organizations, what suggestions can be offered for improving the management of external and internal political forces? Pfeffer and Salancik (1978) provide examples of strategies used by individual companies and groups of companies to manage external dependencies and pressures. They divide these into three broad categories: altering organizational interdependence, establishing collective structures of interorganizational action, and controlling interdependence through law and social sanction (1978, pp. 113–224).

The first of these categories deals generally with organizational growth and the related topics of mergers and diversification. Their basic argument, supported by a number of empirical studies, is that firms can use merger and acquisition to deal with their critical dependencies by merging into the industries on which they are the most dependent for resources (Pfeffer and Salancik, 1978, p. 123).

In discussing growth as a strategy for reducing an organization's dependence on powerful influencers, they suggest that growth may allow the organization to absorb parts of the environment on which it is dependent. However, in some cases, it may actually increase dependence by increasing the organization's need for capital (Pfeffer and Salancik, 1978, p. 139).

The second category, collective structures of interorganizational action, deals with joint ventures, interlocking boards of directors, trade associations, coalitions, and cartels. The authors state that these sorts of techniques allow organizations to exchange information and obtain commitments from each other so they can plan more predictably (Pfeffer and Salancik, 1978, p. 144).

In the final category, they state that the use of laws and social sanctions typically includes either or both of two functions: (1) election activity and (2) government activity, which involves attempts to influence government decisionmakers and to mold public opinion (Pfeffer and Salancik, 1978, p. 217).

Sexty (1980) discusses strategies used by Canadian state-owned firms (or Crown companies) to increase their autonomy from government control or influence in strategic decision making. These autonomy strategies include creating distinctive corporate identities, sharing ownerships, debt financing in private markets, and seeking regulation through administrative tribunals.

Managements of state-owned enterprises seek to create distinctive identities through advertisements and statements in annual reports which de-emphasize the company's link with the government and with day-to-day government politics. This serves to facilitate independence of management from government interference. Some

Crown companies may seek to sell shares to small private investors in order to reduce the influence of the government. In *Power In and Around Organizations* (1983), Mintzberg notes that as ownership becomes disbursed, each shareholder has proportionally less power. Sexty points out that once minority shareholders exist, the company is responsible to ensure their return on investment. Governments must then carefully consider the effects of their directives on minority shareholders, which may reduce their tendency to interfere with the management of the Crown corporations (1980, p. 378).

Seeking debt financing may be another way of reducing government influence by forcing governments to carefully consider the effects of their actions on the company's credit rating. Finally, some Crown corporations favor review by an administrative tribunal rather than by politicians themselves because it is often easier to establish a relationship with such a tribunal. Also, such a tribunal may form a buffer between the company and the government on sensitive political issues.

Intelligent use of these influence strategies requires that managers have a clear understanding of the demands placed on them, the sources of these demands, and the power behind each. One means of gaining this understanding is through Strategic Assumptions Analysis, which has been described by Mason and Mitroff (1981) and is based on notions of stakeholder analysis discussed earlier in this book (see chapter 4). The use of this technique may allow divergent points of view by diverse stakeholders to be represented in strategic decisions.

To aid managers in responding more effectively to environmental pressures for increased social responsibility, there are a number of techniques or strategies for integrating social responsibility into strategic management (Carroll and Hoy, 1984). Carroll and Hoy discuss several examples of attempts made by corporations to integrate social responsibility into their strategic management.

A good example of politically based strategy recommendations is Quinn's work on logical incrementalism. His book *Strategies for Change* contains prescriptions for influencing the social, behavioral, and political processes involved in strategic management. He states that good managers do not follow formal procedures in formulating strategies. Instead, they blend analytical and political techniques to create commitment to evolving strategies (Quinn, 1980, p. 98).

Quinn's perspective provides the basis for a number of recommendations aimed at influencing stakeholder groups within the strategic management process. He suggests, for example, that goals should sometimes be vague and general rather than specific. Specific goals that are clearly and widely announced may provide a focus for opposition and create excessive centralization and rigidity. Quinn offers recommendations for managing the politicized "logical incremental" approach to strategic management. He suggests that executives establish information networks to amplify understanding of issues, use symbolic gestures to build credibility, build support or "pockets of commitment" for strategic change, use trial concepts, manage coalitions, and empower project champions.

Quinn also suggests that executives must work to build awareness of the need for change and create commitment to change through the manipulation of symbols within the organization. The assessment of the demands and power of stakeholders is an essential first step in any attempt to manage them. Channon discusses the Social Response Matrix as a way of representing stakeholder interests (Channon, 1979). Wilson's concepts of intensity-diffusion and convergence provide a means of classifying future demands of stakeholder groups. Using these concepts, it is possible to develop an assessment of the intensity of demands at the present time and the likelihood that these demands will become more intense in the future (Wilson, 1974).

Stakeholders exist within as well as outside the organization. The assessment of an organization's culture provides one way of determining the most powerful internal stakeholder groups. Those who develop new strategies must be sure they are consistent with the demands of stakeholder groups and with the company's culture. The Cultural Risk Matrix developed by Schwartz and Davis allows management to assess the compatibility between a new strategy and a company's existing culture (Schwartz and Davis, 1981).

MacMillan (1978, pp. 105–112) develops a prescriptive framework for analyzing the political allies and opponents in each critical decision area and formulating strategy on the basis of this analysis. Political strategy formulation involves the selection of allies, negotiation with key allies, and the formulation of offensive and defensive strategies. MacMillan's book is useful in that it points out key issues that must be considered in dealing with the political aspects of strategic management. However, MacMillan's recommendations may not take full account of the ambiguity, complexity, and ill-structuredness of political strategy formulation. It is extremely difficult to assess the internal political structures of one's own organization, which may change rapidly.

Using Multiple Strategic Decision Aids

Executives' analysis of their own decisions' shortcomings will determine the type of normative prescriptions they use in improving future decisions. If they feel past failures were due to a lack of understanding, they will tend to choose those recommendations in table 5–1 consistent with model I. If they feel the failures were due to inadequacies in the formulation process, they will choose recommendations grounded in model II assumptions. If they feel past failures were due to imperfect representation of stakeholders or clumsy management of political processes, they will choose model III recommendations. In this chapter, I have summarized a number of approaches to improving decisions that may be useful to practitioners interested in learning more about normative prescriptions in each of the three categories.

It is a mistake to view these prescriptions as substitutes for each other. All decisions are influenced to some extent by cognitive, organizational, *and* political processes. The failure to recognize this fact may in itself be a cause of decisional failure. All three perspectives must be combined in order to ensure that complex strategic problems are thoroughly understood and properly solved.

I have put off discussing the integration of the three perspectives on strategic decision making until I could discuss the prescriptions consistent with each perspective. However, it is now time to consider how the three perspectives may be combined. This integration will provide the basis for integrative suggestions for improving strategic decisions. Figure 5–1 shows, in diagrammatic form, the way these three perspectives can be integrated.

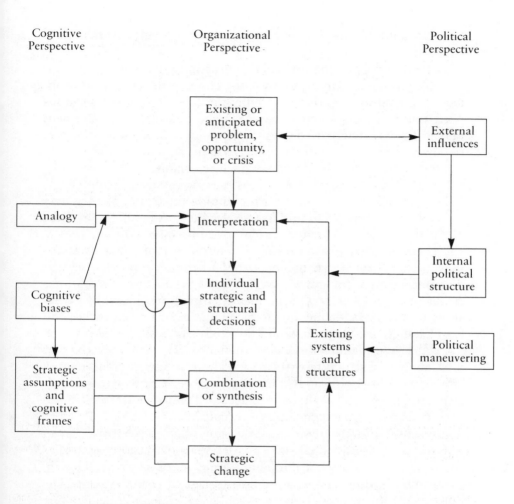

Note: Arrows indicates direction of influence.

Figure 5–1. *Integrating the Three Perspectives*

The Organizational Perspective

The material from the organizational perspective deals with the process of decision making and the way organizations adapt to new environmental demands through streams of multiple decisions. These streams of decisions produce either successful or unsuccessful adaptation to the environment through both strategic and structural changes.

The first part of the flowchart model in figure 5–1 is the stimulus for strategic adaptation that may come in the form of a problem, opportunity, or crisis (Mintzberg et al., 1976). This stimulus need not involve an actual environmental change. Management may anticipate new environmental demands that have not yet materialized and these may be the basis for strategic decisions.

Individual strategic decisions are then made to deal with the stimulus. These individual decisions may be tightly coordinated as is recommended in the normative planning literature, or they may be relatively independent and loosely coupled, as described in some of the literature on incremental planning processes (Quinn, 1980).

There are two basic ways coordination of individual decisions may be achieved. First, independent individual decisions may be combined into a company's overall strategic posture. Second, the major strategic posture may be identified first and individual decisions necessary to define and implement the strategic posture follow. Changes in structure would be a part of this strategic posture.

If decision making is not coordinated, then small-scale changes in strategy and structure will occur without reference to an overall strategic plan or posture. If this happens, the chances of a strategy-structure mismatch would be increased. Of course, existing systems and structures affect each stage of the process.

Since the process of strategic decision making is often cyclical, the outcome of individual strategic decisions may cause strategists to reinterpret the original problem, opportunity, or crisis. This, in turn, could lead to another round of strategic decision making. The outcome of this process is strategic change that may affect existing systems and structures.

The Cognitive Perspective

Cognitive processes and structures of key decisionmakers affect strategic decisions and adaptation in a number of ways. Analogies to familiar events or situations may be used to define new problems, opportunities, or crises.

Cognitive biases may affect the choice of analogies in problem definition. They will also influence the way individual strategic problems are formulated, the range of alternatives considered, and the decisions' outcomes. Finally, cognitive biases will affect strategists' assumptions and cognitive frames. Because of these biases, assumptions and frames may not take all relevant information into account and they may be inappropriately simplistic.

Strategic assumptions and cognitive frames will influence initial interpretation of environmental stimuli and subsequent decision making. Assumptions and frames may also affect the way individual strategic decisions are combined or synthesized. Alternatively, strategic decisions may lead to the modification of assumptions and the creation of new frames.

The Political Perspective

Political processes interact with and shape cognitive processes in strategic adaptation. External influencers may create the stimuli for strategic adaptation. Real or anticipated changes in the desires or demands of these influencers may provide the basis for changes in the internal political structure and power bases. Alternatively, changes in the environment may create changes in the power of external influencers, which is then reflected in the internal political structure. If this structure is relatively simple and free of conflict, interpretation of the environmental stimulus and subsequent decision making may occur without significant political maneuvering.

However, if political maneuvering does occur, characteristics of the internal political structure determine its processes and outcomes. Political maneuvering impacts individual decision making, the combination of these decisions into an intended strategy, and the translation of this intended strategy into a realized strategy.

Developing Integrated Prescriptions

From the preceding figure and discussion, it is clear that cognitive and political factors can influence the organizational process of strategic decision making in negative ways. Cognitive, organizational, and political factors may all work together to support a particular *strategic orientation* for a company and to make it extremely difficult for this orientation to change. Individuals in the organization may initially perceive that their political ends are served by a particular strategic orientation. As the strategic orientation solidifies, new organizational structures and processes develop that reinforce the orientation by defining organizational roles in terms of the new orientation and by providing information that supports the new orientation and causes decisionmakers to frame individual problems in terms of the overall strategic orientation. Cognitive factors come into play as decisionmakers' conceptions of and solutions to new strategic issues are shaped by existing organizational structures and processes. These points are discussed in greater detail by Lyles and Schwenk (1986).

A principle is needed by which the political and cognitive aspects of strategic decision making can be used to *increase* rather than decrease the quality of decisions. The principle I will use for this purpose is the principle of *structured conflict*. Differences between decisionmakers must be clearly identified and debated in some structured way.

One way of introducing structured conflict is to use some form of devil's advocacy to promote dialogue or debate between stakeholder groups. Devil's advocacy involves the formal or informal presentation of alternative views of strategic problems to those responsible for formulating strategies. There is evidence that this process improves understanding of strategic problems (Schwenk, 1984c; Mason and Mitroff, 1981). Thus devil's advocacy is an organizational process by which the political interests of stakeholders can be used to improve cognitive processes and understanding. This sort of devil's advocacy has been used informally with great success in a number of companies and has been incorporated into formal strategic decision aids (Schwenk, 1985a).

Because of the importance of the principles of devil's advocacy and structured conflict, they will be discussed at length in the next chapter. In the concluding chapter, I will discuss the use of structured conflict to integrate diverse perspectives in strategic decision making.

6
Structured Conflict and Devil's Advocacy in Strategic Decision Making

> What kills spontaneous fictions, what recalls the impassioned fancy from its improvisations, is the angry voice of some contrary fancy. Nature, silently making fools of us all our lives, never would bring us to our senses; but the maddest assertions of the mind may do so, when they challenge one another. (George Santayana, *Skepticism and Animal Faith*, 1923, p. 8)

Conflicting views exist in all organizations. Often these are based on different political interests. When representatives of different political interest groups or those with different perspectives on strategic issues confront each other in structured discussion or debate, decision making may be improved in a number of ways.

Research on structured conflict suggests that through its use, cognitive processes may be improved, resulting in greater mastery of information and understanding of the decision as well as less bolstering of one's own view in the face of conflicting evidence. Interpersonal and organizational processes may be improved, resulting in greater information exchange. Political factors may be improved, resulting in a greater understanding of others' points of

Some of the material in this chapter appeared in an earlier paper in the *Journal of Management Studies*, 1984, *21*, 153–168.

view and incorporation of others' information into the final decision (Johnson and Tjosvold, 1983; Mason and Mitroff, 1981; Tjosvold, 1985).

In this chapter, I will discuss research on the effects of diversity
and disagreement on strategic decision making as well as the use of
structured conflict through devil's advocacy. I will then offer recommendations for combining multiple perspectives through the use
of devil's advocacy.

One factor that is a necessary precondition for structured conflict is a difference of opinions or views between organizational
members. One group of researchers has examined the relationship between consensus among decisionmakers and organizational
performance.

Bourgeois (1985, p. 564) collected information on the perceptions of environmental uncertainty and organizational goals of
ninety-nine top-level executives in twenty firms. He found that consensus on perceived environmental uncertainty and goal consensus
were associated with lower financial performance. He also found
that diversity of views was positively correlated with overall accuracy of the perception of environmental uncertainty within firms.

These results extend those of an earlier study by Bourgeois
(1980). Using data from interviews with twelve CEOs and questionnaire responses by sixty-seven top-level executives, he determined that disagreement on goals and agreement on means were
associated with higher performance, whereas agreement on goals
and disagreement on means led to the worst performance.

De Woot, Heyvaert, and Martou (1977, p. 66) found that companies that had a heterogeneity of orientation and frequent disagreement made better decisions regarding strategic change.
Grinyer and Norburn (1977) found that high levels of disagreement
among top executives was related to high performance.

Taken as a whole, these studies suggest that diversity and disagreement may improve perceptions of the environment and the
quality of decision making. Diversity of organizational members
seems to produce differences in goals that is associated with higher
performance.

Structured conflict is not a specific technique but rather a *gen-*

eral approach or orientation toward decision making in organizations. It provides a way of combining decision aids from different perspectives in strategic decision making. This approach to combining decision aids has been chosen as a basis for my recommendations because research has shown that structured conflict has beneficial effects on decisions.

However, before developing my recommendations, I will discuss the results of research on various forms of structured conflict. This discussion will provide background for the recommendations. Within this discussion, I will describe the criteria by which the different approaches to structured conflict were evaluated.

The term *devil's advocacy* has often been used to describe structured conflict in business decisions. Though each theorist has a slightly different definition of the role a devil's advocate should play, there is fundamental agreement that the role should involve the formal introduction of dissent into decision-making processes in which premature consensus inhibits the challenging of assumptions and the consideration of a range of alternatives. The following sections of the chapter will describe some of the more common variants of this approach.

In the next section, alternative definitions of the devil's advocate procedure by its proponents in business and public policy will be examined as a basis for the development of a more detailed definition than is found in most discussions of the process. Next, the empirical research on the effectiveness of this approach will be reviewed. There is a stream of laboratory and field research in the management literature that has implications for the use of devil's advocates in managerial decision making. Finally, based on this research, recommendations for improving the effectiveness of devil's advocates will be offered.

Alternative Conceptions of Devil's Advocacy

There are significant differences in terminology among the authors who have discussed the use of devil's advocates. Though they all agree that the devil's advocates introduce conflict in order to improve decision making, they differ on the point at which devil's advocates should intervene in the decision process, the role the devil's advocates should play, the types of support the devil's advocates should have, and whether or not the role should be rotated among organizational members. In this section, the devil's advocate technique and its major variants will be discussed. At the end of this section, the major differences in the conceptions of the technique will be outlined.

Simple Devil's Advocacy

Techniques and Advantages. In recommending the use of devil's advocates by policymakers, Janis (1972) and Janis and Mann (1977) use Robert F. Kennedy's role in the Cuban Missile Crisis as an example of its successful use. They suggest that in situations in which there is a great deal of agreement among policymakers and there is danger of premature consensus, the chief executive should assign one or more group members to the role of devil's advocate. This person should "be given an unambiguous assignment to present his arguments as cleverly and convincingly as he can, like a good lawyer, challenging the testimony of those advocating the majority position." Janis suggests that this person should introduce much-needed controversy by raising issues in a conventional low-key style (1972, p. 215).

Herbert and Estes (1977) discuss the use of devil's advocates as a way of formalizing dissent in the executive decision process. The authors suggest that they would be most helpful in major strategic decisions in turbulent environments where outcome criteria for the decision are subjective or value-laden (1977, p. 665). They suggest that an individual, either within or outside the organization, should be appointed to the position of devil's advocate for every major organizational decision.

The devil's advocate should begin with the formal statement of a proposed course of action and the analysis underlying the proposal. He should then examine the proposal for inconsistencies, inaccuracies, and irrelevancies and prepare a critique of the proposal based on this examination. If the proposal is found to be unsound, the devil's advocate should develop a reanalysis of the problem and alternative recommendations. A kind of confrontation session between an advocate of the original proposal and the devil's advocate is then held with key organizational decisionmakers as observers. Based on this confrontation session, the organizational decision-makers can then accept the proposal, modify it, or develop a completely new proposal based on a more complete understanding of the original proposal's shortcomings.

Either organizational members or external consultants may play the role of devil's advocates. If organizational members are used, Herbert and Estes suggest that the role should be rotated among junior executives with upper-management potential (1977, p. 666). The devil's advocate was a key factor enabling President Kennedy and his advisors to avoid groupthink in the latter case.

Jervis (1968, 1976) suggests that in order for devil's advocates to be effective, decisionmakers must have "a willingness to play with material from different angles and in the context of unpopular as well as popular hypotheses" (1968, pp. 464–65). They should also select subordinates so that they have conflicting policy preferences. The purpose of the devil's advocate(s) is to promote this willingness and encourage decisionmakers to think more carefully about the beliefs and images that underlie their policies (1976, p. 416).

De Rivera (1968) suggests that a subgroup within the policymaking group be assigned to elicit the assumptions underlying a given policy and help the group critically examine these assumptions. This subgroup should actively collect information contrary to the proposed plan or policy, remain sensitive to unpopular views, and periodically present the most reasonable possible case for alternative beliefs and plans to policymakers. The subgroup should be composed of competent people who have the trust of top decisionmakers and are loyal to them. They should be given periodic opportunities to present their case to decisionmakers and they should receive feedback to assure that the leadership understands the case they have presented (de Rivera, 1968, pp. 62–63).

Cosier (1981, p. 647) develops a model of the devil's advocate critique process involving the identification of assumptions underlying a recommended strategy, the development of a critique of these assumptions, the production of an alternative strategy based on this critique, and the choice of a final strategy after a debate between the proponents of the recommended strategy and the proponents of the critique.

Cosier's Devil's Advocate Planning Model begins with a recommended strategy for an organization and involves the development of a critique that explicitly identifies and criticizes the assumptions underlying the original plan. This critique forms the basis for the development of a revised plan based on alternative assumptions that should be clearly articulated. This revised plan may then be subjected to another devil's advocate critique if this is deemed appropriate.

Schwenk and Huff (1986) seek to provide information on informal devil's advocacy by examining naturally occurring conflict or argumentation in a budgetary decision involving a group of high-level public school administrators. The authors recorded meetings of those administrators in which the budgetary decision was discussed and made transcripts of these recordings. The researchers each read the transcripts involved and identified all cases of devil's advocacy. While there were problems with definitively identifying these cases, several dozen clear examples of devil's advocacy were found in the transcripts. According to Schwenk and Huff, these administrators primarily used devil's advocacy to challenge and define three basic types of assumptions: assumptions about data, assumptions about stakeholders, and assumptions about goals and values. They offer several observations about devil's advocacy as it exists in established groups of decisionmakers.

1. The devil's advocate function is widely dispersed among group members.

2. In some cases, individuals serve as their own devil's advocate. In other cases, individuals take on a position that another member of the group is known to support and that the speaker is known to generally disagree with.

3. In general, argumentation is contained and often includes disclaimers.

4. Within a single discussion, the process of argumentation often does not lead to a conclusion. Rather it becomes part of the data-gathering process.

Problems with Simple Devil's Advocacy. Those who discuss devil's advocacy, however, are not unanimous in their praise. Pointing to President Johnson's use of the technique during the Vietnam War, they emphasize that when those in charge of the policy-making process are unable or unwilling to take the devil's advocate's proposals seriously, a variety of problems may arise. The devil's advocates may become "domesticated" (Thompson, 1968) so that their objections are discounted and they lose their effectiveness. George Reedy, for example, suggests that in many established decision-making groups, the devil's advocate's objections and cautions are discounted before they are delivered (1970, p. 11).

One individual in the group studied by Schwenk and Huff provides support for this assertion. This person frequently played the role of devil's advocate. Other group members indicated in individual interviews that his comments were often "off-base," but his input was considered useful for stimulating others in the group to think clearly. In the budget meetings, when this person brought up an objection to a particular budget cut, other members of the group generally responded to answer his objection and demonstrate that it did not have merit. As a result, very few of his statements were actually reflected in the final recommendations for budget cuts.

It might be argued that this particular devil's advocate had been neutralized. However, this person was very valuable in convincing decisionmakers that they had behaved rationally and had considered a wide range of perspectives and alternatives. In a decision process in which participants want to behave comprehensively, few objections can be totally ignored. As the other decisionmakers articulated the reasons for rejecting the devil's advocate's points, they discovered and clarified their assumptions and developed consensus on these. This suggests that devil's advocates can serve a useful function even when their suggestions are not often reflected in the final decision (Schwenk and Huff, 1986).

Schlaim also suggests that devil's advocates may be subject to severe pressures to conform if their superiors are unwilling to consider alternative views. He cites the example of Joachim von Ribbentrop, Hitler's foreign minister, who had an unshakable conviction that Great Britain would never go to war against Germany. He warned all members of his staff, "If it came to my notice that anyone had expressed a contrary opinion I would kill him myself in his office, and take responsibility before the Fuhrer for it" (Schlaim 1976, pp. 374–75). Mason (1969) suggests that, while devil's advocates may be of some value, they tend to become negative "carping critics" who do not offer constructive alternatives to the strategic recommendations they criticize and may be very demoralizing to decisionmakers. For this reason, a number of variants on devil's advocacy have been developed.

Multiple Advocacy

George (1972) discusses the use of devil's advocates and a related procedure, multiple advocacy, in foreign policy making. George claims that multiple advocacy should be superior to the use of devil's advocates because it includes more advocates and more options. In the multiple advocacy system, representatives of several minority opinions and unpopular views present these to decisionmakers in order to encourage them to question the assumptions underlying the prevailing or favored policy. Simple devil's advocacy typically involves only a single critic of the favored policy.

A key role in this process is that of the *custodian* of unpopular views. The custodian attempts to assure (George, 1972, p. 759):

that there is no major maldistribution of resources among the proponents of various views (important resources include: power, influence, competence, information, analytical resources, and bargaining and persuasion skills);

that there is no involvement by the top-level decisionmaker(s) in the debate;

that there is adequate time for give and take.

Multiple advocacy, like devil's advocacy, is most useful in "novel situations in which important values are at stake but which cannot, or should not, be dealt with by selecting one of the standard responses from the organization's available repertoire" (1972, p. 763).

Dialectical Inquiry

Mason and Mitroff (1981) have developed an alternative technique designed as an improvement on simple devil's advocacy. They call this technique *dialectical inquiry* and, in its elaborated form, *strategic assumptions analysis*. Dialectical inquiry includes techniques for choosing individuals to form groups that will produce the most divergent solutions to strategic problems. These techniques involve, first, the assessment of the personality and problem-solving orientation of each person in the decision-making group. Decisionmakers are then clustered into groups that are maximally homogeneous and also maximally different from each other. The groups then develop alternatives to a recommended strategy or plan by identifying assumptions upon which it is based and upon which the group members do not agree. If groups with conflicting policy preferences already exist, as is often the case, these may be used and it is not necessary to use the procedure for forming divergent groups.

An important part of the dialectical inquiry technique is the explicit identification of the most important or *pivotal* assumptions, those assumptions providing the foundation for the strategy and on which there is the strongest disagreement (Mason and Mitroff, 1981, p. 49). Since the time of key decisionmakers is valuable, it is important that they do not waste time evaluating assumptions that are not critical to the strategy or assumptions on which there is little disagreement. After a debate between alternative plans, these assumptions are then discussed and negotiated in order to arrive at a common assumption pool.

Dialectical inquiry requires the development of explicit counterplans based on different assumptions than the favored plan as the basis for a dialectical debate. However, a devil's advocate does not have to develop an explicit counterplan. If a favored strategy has been identified early in the decision-making process, the techniques for constructing divergent groups and identifying pivotal assumptions could be used as a basis for constructing a critique that merely challenges the key assumptions but offers no alternative plan.

Major Differences

An examination of the discussions of alternative forms of devil's advocacy reveals a number of significant differences in their descriptions of the process. There is general agreement that devil's advocates should introduce conflict by challenging previously formed assumptions and alternatives. However, there is disagreement on how this can best be done.

One difference has to do with the point at which the devil's advocate should intervene in the process. Herbert and Estes argue that the devil's advocate should intervene *after* a proposal has been developed and should prepare a counterplan if the situation warrants it. This view is shared by Cosier and de Rivera. However, Janis and Mann as well as George suggest this intervention should occur *throughout* the decision process.

A second point of difference has to do with whether or not devil's advocates should focus on critiquing the majority position or whether they should actively advocate alternative views. Cosier (1981) suggests that the devil's advocate should focus on the critique of the favored plan rather than the development of a counterplan. Jervis, Herbert and Estes, and de Rivera also suggest a focus on the critique of favored policies but suggest that advocating alternative policies may be appropriate under some circumstances.

George as well as Mason and Mitroff, in their improvements on devil's advocacy, explicitly suggest that counterplans should be identified. Mason and Mitroff have developed techniques for choosing members of the decision-making group to prepare counterplans, while George's custodian's primary function is to ensure that those representing opposing perspectives or counterplans are given the resources to effectively advocate them.

Finally, these authors differ on the question of whether or not the devil's advocate role should be assumed by a single person or group permanently or whether it should be rotated among group members. Janis and Mann as well as de Rivera imply that it should be assumed by a single group member over a long time frame. George's custodian role is also a long-term role. However, the critics of devil's advocacy point out that this may lead to domestication of devil's advocates and a reduction in their effectiveness. Herbert and Estes suggest that the role should be rotated among organizational members as a form of management training.

Previous Research on the Effectiveness of Devil's Advocacy and Related Techniques

Though there are significant differences between simple devil's advocacy, dialectical inquiry, and multiple advocacy, the three will be discussed as variants of the basic devil's advocate approach in the remainder of the chapter. The basic devil's advocate procedure is defined here simply as a procedure involving the use of one or more persons to raise objections to favored strategies, challenge assumptions underlying them, and possibly point out alternatives.

In this section of the chapter, the research on the variants of devil's advocacy will be discussed as a basis for the development of recommendations for its effective use. There have been a number of field and laboratory experiments reported in the strategic management literature on dialectical inquiry (DI), which involves the development of an explicit counterplan, compared to a very simplified form of devil's advocacy called the DA, which involves only the development of a critique within an explicit counterplan. This research can be of value to managers desiring direction in the effective use of devil's advocates.

Mason (1969), who developed descriptions of the techniques based on the work of Churchman (1966), suggested that the DI should be more effective at exposing underlying assumptions than the DA because the DI involves the generation of constructive alternatives, while the devil's advocate in the DA merely plays the role of an adverse and often carping critic of the favored plan or recommendation. Thus, he suggests that the DA does not assist in the development of a new set of assumptions or a new world view.

However, both the DA and DI approaches are, according to Mason (1969), distinctly superior to what he calls the expert (E) approach, which is seen as the most common approach to top management decision making. In this approach, members of a planning department or consultants provide expert advice and recommendations regarding the plans the organization should follow. Mason suggests that the planning recommendations contain hidden assumptions that are very frequently not communicated to management, but that may reinforce management biases. This is one of the most critical drawbacks to this approach (1969, pp. B406–7).

The DI has been used as an aid to corporate decision making in a number of field experiments. Mason (1969) studied the effects of the DI on strategic decision making in an abrasives manufacturing company. He obtained a strategic planning document from the company's planning department, identified its ten underlying assumptions, and constructed a counterplan based on opposite assumptions. The plan and counterplan were then presented to management in a structured debate. Mason reported that the company's managers were more satisfied with the strategy they developed as a result of using the DI. They felt it led to a "new encompassing view" of the planning problem, to the identification of key assumptions, and to the generation of new alternatives.

In a public-sector application, Mitroff, Barabba, and Kilmann (1977) used the DI on a planning problem at the Bureau of the Census in Washington, D.C. A total of 120 Bureau of the Census employees were given a lecture on the DI. Forty-five of the employees decided to participate in the next stage of the study and were then clustered into five homogenous groups. These groups then produced planning reports suggesting new future directions for the bureau—reports differing significantly from one another. Next, the assumptions underlying each report were identified and debated. Finally, representatives from each group formed an executive group that produced a final integrative report. According to Mitroff et al., this report contained several interesting ideas about the Bureau of the Census's role in the year 2000 and several alternatives that the participants found innovative and exciting.

Emshoff and Finnel developed a more detailed procedure for applying the DI to strategic planning that they called *strategic assumptions analysis*. This technique contains (in addition to the dialectical debate on assumptions) an *assumption negotiation* phase.

This phase occurs after decisionmakers have been divided into groups and the groups have generated two or more plans based on different interpretations of the organizational data base. As part of the assumption negotiation phase, members of each group are required to identify and question assumptions from the other groups that are "most perturbing to the group's policy—those assumptions which are hardest for each group to live with" (1978, p. 11). These are then discussed and negotiated in order to arrive at a common assumption pool. Thus, strategic assumptions analysis involves the generation of both counterplans and critiques.

Emshoff and Finnel examined the effects of strategic assumptions analysis in a company that they called Basic Materials. A planning group at the company used the technique to revise a strategic plan they had developed. The authors concluded that strategic assumptions analysis assured a more thorough analysis of the data and produced a revised strategy that was superior to the initial strategy (1978, p. 30).

Strategic assumptions analysis was applied by Mitroff, Emshoff, and Kilmann (1979) to a pricing decision in a drug company. Here, the managers had divided themselves into three groups, each of which advocated a different pricing policy. There was considerable conflict in the decision-making group from the beginning. Therefore, it was not necessary to use any special procedures to formulate divergent groups. The consultants entered the decision-making process at its beginning and focused their attention on clarifying the assumptions between groups. Through the use of strategic assumptions analysis, these three groups of managers examined their divergent assumptions and negotiated to arrive at a common assumption pool that was the basis for agreement on a final pricing policy. The authors reported that this procedure produced more and better alternatives and led to a different pricing policy than the one that would have been chosen had it not been used.

Thus, the field research provides some support for the assertion that the DI is effective in helping managers deal with ill-structured problems. It deepens decisionmakers' understanding of a problem, reduces the narrowing effects of expert advice, leads to the generation of new alternatives, and increases decisionmakers' satisfaction with the decision. However, these conclusions are somewhat tentative since the field studies relied on managerial judgments of the effects of the DI and because they did not include control conditions.

Another line of research has dealt with the value of conflicting interpretations of data and the comparative effectiveness of the DA approach and, in more controlled settings, DI. In these experiments, the researchers did not attempt to capture the full complexity of devil's advocacy or dialectical inquiry as they were used in the field. Rather, they focused on what they felt was the central feature of the DI, the presentation to decisionmakers of two conflicting interpretations of the same data base through a plan and counterplan. This was compared to the DA format that involved a single interpretation of the data and a critique of this interpretation suggesting no alternative. These experiments involved the presentation of a standardized plan and critique to all DA subjects and a standardized plan and counterplan to all DI subjects.

Cosier (1978) developed E, DA, and DI treatments for a laboratory setting and measured their effects on performance at a multiple-cue probability learning (MCPL) task. The task required individuals to predict criterion values using three cues having a probabilistic relationship to the criterion. Subjects in the E condition received a planning report from an "expert" recommending that they give most weight to one particular cue in making their predictions. This, according to Mason, represented the most common approach to organizational decisionmaking, the expert (E) approach. Subjects in the DA condition received this same "expert" report plus a critique that questioned the assumptions of the first report but offered no alternative recommendations, a treatment incorporating the essential elements of the DA as described by Mason (1969). Subjects in the DI condition were given the "expert" report plus a counterplan suggesting an alternate set of cue weightings.

All subjects made twenty predictions in each of three distinct contexts or "states of the world." In the first world state, the cue-criterion relationship was consistent with the recommendations of the expert report. In the third world state, the relationship was consistent with the counterproposal. The second world state represented a compromise between the proposal and the counterproposal. Cosier found that in the third world state, the DA subjects made significantly more accurate predictions than the E or DI subjects. Thus, the results of this study tended to favor the DA.

Later laboratory studies by Cosier, Ruble, and Aplin (1978), Cosier (1980), and Schwenk and Cosier (1980) using a similar experimental design have generally shown that compared to the simpler E approach, the DA and the DI improve the ability of subjects to discover the relationship between cues and a criterion and employ that relationship in making predictions. However, the DA appeared to be more effective than the DI.

Schwenk (1982) examined the effects of decisionmakers' ambiguity tolerance and a combined critique and counterplan (DA/DI) treatment on performance at the MCPL task. He found that for decisionmakers high in ambiguity tolerance, the DA/DI led to better prediction performance than an E, DA, or DI treatment alone. However, only the superiority of the DA/DI to the E was statistically significant, while the superiority of the DA/DI to the DI was marginally significant. Schwenk (1984a), using the MCPL task and student subjects, showed that the DI treatment was more effective than the DA for subjects who were highly involved in the decision-making task, while the DA was more effective for subjects lower in commitment to the task. Schweiger and Finger (1984) found no significant differences between subjects given the DA or DI treatment in an MCPL task—a finding that is difficult to reconcile with the results of nearly all other MCPL studies.

The DA and DI have also been examined using case analysis tasks and simulations. Schwenk and Thomas (1983) showed that the DA/DI treatment improved the cost effectiveness of solutions and reduced the tendency to collect too much information in a group of managers working on a business case. Schwenk (1984b) investigated the effects of the DA and DI as well as the medium through which they were presented on decisionmakers' generation of alternatives and final choice of a recommendation. He found that the DA treatment, presented in written rather than oral form, led to the generation of more strategic alternatives than the DI or E approaches presented in written form. Also, the DA reduced the effects of an expert report on decisionmakers' final recommendations more than did the DI. However, both the DA and DI were perceived by subjects to be more valuable than the E.

Cosier and Rechner (1985) showed that a DA treatment was more useful than a DI treatment for student subjects making decisions in a business simulation. However, the DA was not found to be more effective than the DI with a group of experienced managers using the same simulation.

Schweiger, Sandberg, and Ragan (1986) showed that both DA and DI treatments increased the quality of assumptions and recommendations when compared to a consensus approach in a laboratory experiment involving a case analysis task and groups of MBAs. In this experiment, the DI was superior to the DA in terms of the quality of assumptions surfaced. However, subjects given the consensus treatment expressed more satisfaction and desire to continue working with their groups as well as greater acceptance of their groups' decisions. This suggests that there may be some negative consequences of the conflict generated by the DA and DI.

In summary, the field and laboratory research strongly support the effectiveness of different forms of devil's advocacy over the more common approaches to organizational decision making that do not involve the introduction of conflict. The field research demonstrates that decisionmakers who use an approach to devil's advocacy that involves the generation of explicit counterplans (the DI) feel it improves their decisions over the expert-based approach they had been using previously. They report that it improves their analysis of data and their understanding of a problem as well as the quality of their solution.

The laboratory research shows that the simple plan/critique format of the DA approach improves decision making over the traditional expert-based approach. It reduces the narrowing effect of expert advice, increases the number of strategic alternatives generated, and improves decisionmakers' use of ambiguous environmental information in making predictions.

However, those who have argued against the use of devil's advocates correctly point out that, in some cases, their use has not led to increased representation of critical stakeholder interests and has not prevented disastrous errors. Therefore, it is necessary to clarify the proper role of devil's advocates and establish realistic expectations for their effectiveness. It is also necessary to draw suggestions from the research for making devil's advocates as effective as possible in situations where their use is appropriate.

The Necessity of Serious Commitment to Devil's Advocacy

For devil's advocates to have any impact on decisions, their role must be valued and their objections taken seriously. Without such commitment, the devil's advocate may serve merely to reassure decisionmakers that they have heard both sides of an issue. They may attempt to domesticate those playing the role of devil's advocate and, failing that, they may exclude them from decision making.

In order for decisionmakers to take the devil's advocate seriously, they must admit that there are multiple ways of viewing a problem and that the assumptions underlying their own view may not be correct. As Mason (1969, p. 413) suggested, management must acknowledge "that there may exist multiple interpretations of the data" relevant to a decision.

The factors influencing this willingness have not been discussed at length in the literature. However, it seems that decisionmakers' ambiguity tolerance (their ability to deal with ambiguous information from the environment) may be one factor (Schwenk, 1982). A second factor may have to do with decisionmakers' prior experience. Failure in the Bay of Pigs invasion may have led President Kennedy to be more humble about his decision-making abilities and to take the statements of his devil's advocates more seriously. During the escalation decisions in the Vietnam War, President Johnson had no analogous failure experience to promote his serious consideration of the suggestions of devil's advocates (Bill Moyer and George Ball).

The structure or culture of the organization may also determine the probability that devil's advocates will be helpful. In groups or organizations in which there is a single dominant view *and* where this view is strongly defended in response to perceived external threat, decisionmakers may find it difficult to really question their assumptions as the devil's advocate suggests. However, Janis (1972) and Janis and Mann (1977) point out that such a group may need a devil's advocate or some other technique for breaking down the groupthink that develops as they try to meet a perceived external threat.

Finally, time pressure may be a factor determining how seriously the devil's advocate's advice is taken. Dealing with the comments of devil's advocates requires time and devil's advocates may be ignored by decisionmakers facing a deadline, even though they may need a devil's advocate more under such circumstances (George, 1972, p. 759).

Specific Suggestions for the Use of the Devil's Advocacy

Even if decisionmakers are able to look critically at their assumptions, they may not receive the full benefit of the technique if the devil's advocate does not play the role effectively. Next, I give some suggestions derived from the research for using devil's advocates productively. Caution must be exercised in drawing normative recommendations from the research. However, with this caution in mind, some tentative rules can be advanced.

First, the specific role of the devil's advocate should vary depending on the type of decision. Here, several basic types of decisions will be considered and different recommendations for the use of devil's advocacy will be made depending on the type of decision in which it is to be used. Four basic distinctions will be dealt with. Well-structured decisions will be distinguished from ill-structured decisions. Decisions in which the top-level decisionmakers have little information as compared to their staff analysts will be distinguished from those in which they have more complete information. Decisions that require more input from affected groups will be distinguished from those that do not. Finally, decisions in which there is a great deal of preexisting conflict between members of the decision-making group will be distinguished from those where there is very little.

All the field applications of devil's advocacy discussed earlier involve very complex and ill-structured problems. However, some authors do not specify that the devil's advocate should be used for only some types of organizational decisions. Rather, they imply that it should be used almost routinely in top-management decision making (Janis, 1972; Janis and Mann, 1977). From the preceding discussion of the variants of devil's advocacy, it may be concluded that they will all involve some commitment of time beyond that involved in the more traditional approaches to decision making. Some variations such as DI may involve a great deal of additional time. Since research has not addressed the effects of devil's advocacy on well-structured or routine organizational problems, the technique cannot be recommended as improving the solutions to such problems. Therefore, given the additional time involved in using the technique, it may be that it should be reserved for more complex and ill-structured decisions.

In many organizational decisions, staff analysts may have more detailed information on the data relevant to the decision than do the top-level decisionmakers to whom they report. In such cases, it may be best to appoint to the role of devil's advocate members of the staff group or others in the organization who have a similar level of understanding of the data but have differing assumptions. Mason and Mitroff (1981) discuss techniques that may be used to select such people. The critique and plan can then be debated before management in the manner discussed by Mason (1979) and Cosier (1981). If, on the other hand, top management has a relatively high level of understanding of the data compared to the staff analysts, they may play the devil's advocate role themselves.

In some top-level managerial decisions, the major concern is to improve the quality of data analysis and the rationality of decision making. In others, the major concern may be to better represent the views or demands of groups affected by the decision. It may be that the DI and multiple advocacy, as variants of devil's advocacy, are more effective at achieving this end. By allowing representatives of affected groups to prepare counterplans, and possibly by using a "custodian" (George, 1972) to ensure that they are given resources to develop the counterplan, affected groups' inputs may be elicited more effectively than they are by the simple devil's advocate technique.

When there is a great deal of conflict present initially in groups, and when group members are advocating different positions, devil's advocates should be active throughout the decision-making process (Janis, 1972; Janis and Mann, 1977; de Rivera, 1968). They should attempt to articulate and clarify the differences in assumptions that underlie the differences in recommendations as did the consultants in the Mitroff et al. (1979) study involving the drug company.

Mason and Mitroff (1981) discuss a number of procedures for identifying assumptions through examination of beliefs about stakeholders and for identifying the pivotal assumptions that are the fundamental premises of each group's recommendations (1981, pp. 43–49). However, a devil's advocate familiar with the organization's operations may be able to identify these without the help of special techniques.

The devil's advocate in this situation may also be required to play a role similar to that of George's "custodian" to ensure that each group is assisted in developing its case. A structured debate should then occur in which each group is allowed to present its case with rebuttal from other groups and questions from those who have final responsibility for making the decision. Studies (Mitroff et al., 1977, 1979) have shown that this is effective in clarifying assumptions. If the group must reach consensus, it may be necessary to go through an *assumption negotiation* stage (Mason and Mitroff, 1981, p. 52). If consensus is not required, those with final responsibility for the decision should play a role similar to George's "magistrate" in order to avoid becoming prematurely committed to one position.

If the decision-making process is characterized by too little conflict and a preferred alternative has been identified with too little questioning of assumptions, the devil's advocate should play a different role (Herbert and Estes, 1977; Jervis, 1968, 1976; Cosier, 1981). Here, the devil's advocate will attempt to initiate assumption questioning and problem reformulation by identifying critical assumptions underlying the preferred alternative and using these as the basis for a forcefully presented critique that does not offer a clearly defined alternative. Some of the laboratory research (Cosier, 1978, 1980; Cosier et al., 1978; Schwenk, 1982; Schwenk and Cosier, 1980) seems to suggest that this will be more effective than the development of a specific counterplan. However, it may be, as the proponents of the field studies speculate, that with adequate training or indoctrination of decisionmakers, the plan-counterplan format may be even more effective than the plan-critique format. This has not yet been verified. Finally, if the devil's advocate has the time and resources to develop them, *both* a critique and counterplan may be more effective than either alone (Schwenk, 1982), though Schwenk's research did not show that the combination was more effective than the critique alone.

Second, the devil's advocate should avoid strongly identifying with a particular position and becoming a strongly negative "carping critic." Mason (1969) warned against this as a potential problem with the DA. He also suggested that this sort of devil's advocate may "demoralize" decisionmakers, especially those who proposed the initial plan. Rather, the devil's advocate should play the role of a process consultant interested only in surfacing assumptions and improving decisionmaking. Schwenk and Cosier (1980) showed that a "carping critic" form of the DA treatment did not lead to better use of environmental cues than the E treatment, but that a more objective DA treatment did.

In this sense, the models of the debate process, the philosophical concepts that justify these models, and the detailed techniques for managing debate offered by Mitroff and his colleagues (Mason and Mitroff, 1981; Mitroff and Mason, 1981; Cosier, 1981) may be of value to devil's advocates. They may help to legitimize their role as expert process consultants.

Finally, there is some question about whether a single person should play the role of devil's advocate for a series of decisions or whether this role should rotate among group members. The research has not yet addressed this question. If a single individual plays this role over a series of decisions, that person should, through practice, become a more effective devil's advocate. On the other hand, rotation of the role may give the entire group a clearer understanding of the devil's advocate process and prevent the negative consequences that might result from the identification of a single individual as "*the* devil's advocate."

If a single individual adopts the role, he should attempt to identify another individual in the group whose views on the decision in question diverge from the rest of the group to assist him in preparing the critique. If the role shifts to a different person for each decision, the person selected to play the devil's advocate in a particular case should have the maximum divergence of assumptions from other group members. Mason and Mitroff (1981, pp. 114–19) have described techniques that could be helpful in this selection.

The principles of structured conflict or debate represented by devil's advocacy form the basis for recommendations for improving decisions that incorporate organizational, cognitive, and political factors. If properly structured, this procedure may lead to better representation of external and internal influences or stakeholders and may reduce the negative effects of political maneuvering. It may also reduce the effects of biases on decisionmakers' assumptions and cognitive frames, as well as improve the use of analogy in diagnosing new strategic problems. In the long run, this approach may also lead to improvements in organizational decision processes, systems, and structures.

Conclusion and Implications

The research discussed in this chapter demonstrates that the use of devil's advocacy, broadly defined, can improve strategic decision making if certain rules are followed. Briefly stated, the devil's advocate should play the role of process consultant and/or objective critic of a favored strategy rather than be a "carping critic" identified with a particular alternative strategy. The point at which the devil's advocate intervenes and the specific role he plays should be determined by the characteristics of the specific decision considered.

The one major caution regarding the use of devil's advocates has to do with the attitudes of those in the decision-making group. Devil's advocates should only be used if decisionmakers can honestly question their basic assumptions and if they have a sincere commitment to the devil's advocate process. Without such commitment, the use of devil's advocates may be useless or even harmful.

Based on the research conducted on the variants of devil's advocacy thus far, it is possible to offer some suggestions for its effective use. However, there are a number of questions regarding the use of the technique that have not yet been addressed by research. Some of these are given next.

Future research on devil's advocacy could aid practitioners by focusing on the following questions: (1) How effective is devil's advocacy at improving solutions to relatively well structured and routine problems? (2) Is it cost-effective? (3) How specifically can a top-level decisionmaker play the role of devil's advocate without demoralizing the subordinates who propose the plan? (4) Which of the variants of devil's advocacy or which combination of techniques is most useful in promoting input from groups affected by the decision? (5) When a single member or subgroup plays the role of devil's advocate for a series of decisions, how much does its effectiveness improve as a result of learning the role and how much does it diminish as a result of domestication or an increasing tendency of the group to ignore the devil's advocate's suggestions? Future research on such questions may make it possible to make more detailed recommendations for the effective use of devil's advocacy.

Having outlined the principles of devil's advocacy, it is now possible to discuss the ways these principles may be applied to the integration of prescriptions from the three perspectives discussed earlier. This topic will be covered in the final chapter.

7
Conclusion and Implications for Practice and Research

Historically, the predominant explanatory perspective in strategic management has been consistent with Allison's model I or rational actor model. I have discussed three alternative perspectives and have summarized research consistent with each perspective. I have argued that decisionmakers' choice of techniques for improving strategic decisions will be influenced by the perspective from which they explain them and I have summarized strategic decision aids consistent with each perspective. Strategic decisions are so complex that all the major perspectives are necessary in order to fully understand them. Effective strategic decision making requires an integrative view encompassing all perspectives. I have suggested that this integration can be achieved through the principle of structured conflict embodied in various forms of devil's advocacy. It remains for me to describe the way devil's advocacy can be used to integrate the perspectives and to discuss the implications of these ideas for research.

In the next section of this chapter, I will give an example of a strategic problem and, using this example, I will discuss the specific ways analyses and prescriptions from the three perspectives may be integrated through the use of structured devil's advocacy. In the final section of the chapter, I will discuss a number of research directions suggested by the integrative model developed in chapter 5.

Three Perspectives on the Same Strategic Problem

Given the complexity of strategic issues and the limitations of pre-scriptions from each perspective, managers must exercise judgment in deciding which prescriptions to use under which circumstances. This is the *art* of strategic decision making. Multiple approaches may be useful as a basis for dialogue among the members of the top-level decision-making group.

When a company is faced with a complex strategic problem, some in the organization may view it as primarily a technical prob-lem while others view it as an organizational problem and others as a political problem. Decisionmakers who view it as a technical problem require decision aids consistent with the model I perspec-tive, while those who view it as an organizational problem require model II decision aids and those viewing it as a political problem require model III aids.

Lyles and Schwenk (1986) provide an example to illustrate these points in their discussion of a large consulting firm's response to a decline in revenues caused by changes in the national economy, changes in the market for consulting services, and the rise of com-petitors who offered more specialized consulting services.

According to one of the senior partners of this firm, fundamen-tal changes are taking place in the market for consulting services. In his own words:

> Consulting . . . proliferated dramatically following World War II. The biggest firms were those that developed a working relation-ship with the senior management of a client company and advised on just about everything the client thought they needed advice on. The way in which you really sold the service was to maintain a close personal relationship with the people running divisions and then whenever they needed some outside assistance, they would call you to come and give it. So, firms tended to become all things to all clients. (Lyles and Schwenk, 1986, p. 7)

However, this situation changed during the 1970s:

In this country we faced a new situation toward the end of the decade with regard to the degree of sophistication in management in the use of consultants. There was an incredible MBA group during the 60s and 70s. We went from 5,000 graduates a year in the 60s to 65,000 graduates per year in the 80s. So you have a lot of people who think they know a lot about management, about general management, and about strategic kinds of issues. Secondly, you had a lot of alumni from consulting organizations in industry who understand the consultants—how to select and get results from consultants.

This led to the rise of specialty consultants.

Three key people in our firm started their own thing. They really carved out a niche in the market by picking two areas, just in logistics. They offered those consulting services and that's all. They didn't take on anything else and they had no interest in expanding their firm to take on other kinds of work. (Lyles and Schwenk, 1986, p. 15)

Finally, a downturn in business forced a consideration of what should be done to deal with the strategic problem caused by environmental and market changes:

Our business began to turn down in the latter part of 1981. Then I think more and more people came to the conclusion that it's probably a combination of things—the recession being one. Maybe it became more acceptable to them to make such changes because things were not going as well. Few people said that the reason was because of the way we were structured. Nonetheless since we were going to go about some change because of the strategic changes that we thought were taking place and would be during the 80s, it became easier to convince people that were reluctant that we had better do something. So the recession to that extent played into the hands of those wanting to make change. (Lyles and Schwenk, 1986, p. 16)

Let us consider the sorts of prescriptions that might come from each of the three perspectives on the cause of the downturn in business. Some might view the cause as a lack of understanding in the company about effective strategy in the changing consulting industry. This would suggest the use of a model I decision aid, perhaps Porter's (1980) industry analysis framework. Or, it might suggest that the company's executives need to carefully identify the environmental factors that are changing the competitive dynamics of the industry, perhaps with the aid of a technique such as SPIRE. Finally, this view might suggest that the company needs to recruit consultants who do understand the new competitive structure of the industry and can help the company operate more effectively within it.

Those who view the problem as an organizational problem might suggest structural changes that would allow individual units of the company to focus on more specialized consulting services. They might also suggest changes in organizational planning and decision-making procedures to support this new structure. For example, more decisional autonomy might be given to individual units so that they could more effectively respond to demands for new types of services. Changes in measurement, evaluation, and reward systems might be recommended to reward entrepreneurial activity on the part of these units.

Finally, those who take a political perspective might suggest that stakeholders' wishes be reflected in any change. They might focus on one group of internal stakeholders—the partners of the firm—and suggest that the partners' views be solicited and a solution developed that met the needs of the most powerful partners. This would be seen as necessary in order to ensure commitment to the solution.

Combining Multiple Perspectives in Practice

Of course, each perspective is partially correct, though incomplete. Further, it may be difficult for those with the model I perspective to adequately consider solutions from the model II and III perspectives as well. How are these perspectives to be integrated in order to develop an adequate solution to this problem?

This is where the principles of structured conflict inherent in devil's advocacy may be useful. Figure 7–1 shows, in diagrammatic form, a procedure for combining multiple perspectives using the principle of structured conflict embodied in various forms of devil's advocacy.

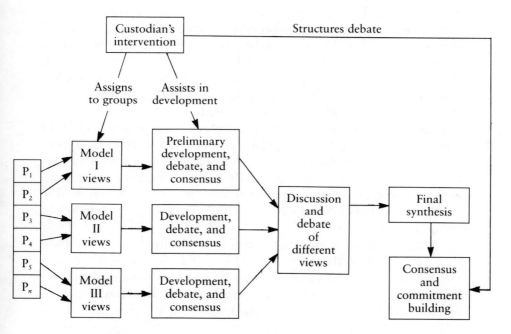

P = Individual perspective on a particular strategic problem.

Figure 7–1. *Combining Multiple Perspectives via the Principle of Structured Conflict Found in Devil's Advocacy*

Individuals with different perspectives on the nature of a strategic problem should first be assigned to groups according to which of the three basic models their view most closely fits. Then, they can determine the implications of their view for the type of decision aids that should be used to solve the problem and the criteria that should be used to evaluate the solution.

Individuals within each cluster should be encouraged to develop the implications of their perspectives by an individual who plays the role of custodian described in chapter 6. This will serve to clarify the prescriptions offered within each perspective and to reduce the number of different perspectives to be considered.

The final alternatives should then be discussed and debated. Techniques and prescriptions from each of the three perspectives can be used to promote the process of devil's advocacy. Model II approaches such as formal environmental scanning may be used to identify and process data relevant to company strategy. Model III techniques can be used to identify the most important stakeholders whose views must be taken into account. Representatives of the stakeholder groups should be encouraged to play the role of devil's advocate and critique the organization's existing strategy. Model I approaches such as the BCG matrix can be used to provide support for the critiques in the process of debate. Techniques such as cognitive mapping can be used to clarify some of the assumptions underlying the existing strategy as well as each critique. When used in this way, recommendations from each of the three perspectives can compliment each other.

The individual or group responsible for the final decision should then attempt to synthesize various views (and the results of the analyses using multiple strategic decision aids). This is admittedly a very difficult task and may not be completely successful. However, even when a true synthesis is not reached, the final strategy should still reflect a broader range of views than it would if this approach was not used.

Mason and Mitroff (1981, pp. 51–52) suggest that when synthesis is difficult to achieve, *assumption negotiation* may be helpful. In this process, decisionmakers recognize the critical assumptions on which they disagree. Each decisionmaker then agrees to relax some of his or her assumptions in exchange for other decisionmakers' relaxing some of their assumptions. This sort of bargaining or negotiation allows a kind of synthesis to be reached despite basic differences in assumptions.

It is possible that the encouragement of controversy through devil's advocacy will reduce morale, commitment to the strategy, and willingness to implement the strategy. Schweiger et al. (1986,

p. 67) found that group members given devil's advocacy and dialectical inquiry treatments expressed less liking for the group and less willingness to work with the group again than those given a consensus-based treatment.

For these reasons, at least one consensus-building session should be held after the final decision is reached. At this session, a number of points should be stressed:

that the individuals arguing for different assumptions and solutions were doing so in order to improve the quality of the decision, not merely to advance their own interests

that it is important for all members of the organization to be committed to the new strategy in order for it to succeed

that differences on this particular strategy problem need not hinder the ability of individuals to work together in the future

Custodians have an active role to play during this part of the process. They must make certain that these points are adequately communicated and understood by all members of the group.

At several points, I have mentioned the role of the custodian. It is appropriate at this point to discuss the role in more detail and to describe the sort of person who should play this role. The custodian should be a person with a fairly high degree of authority and a good knowledge of strategic decisionmaking in the organization. It may be that a single individual could play this role for all major strategic decisions in the organization. Or, the custodian role might be assumed by a different individual for each decision if there is a sufficient number of people who can play this role within the organization. Because of the complexity and importance of this role, it is likely that training in the role would improve a person's performance. Also, it is unlikely that any organization would have a large number of individuals who could play this role effectively. For these reasons, it might be better for a single person to play the role for all major decisions.

In any case, the major responsibilities of the custodian would include all those mentioned in chapter 6:

to ensure that there is no major maldistribution of resources such as information, analytical resources, and influence among the proponents of various views.

to ensure that the top-level decisionmakers who will make the final decision are not actively involved in the development of arguments for a particular point of view or in the debate between points of view.

to ensure that there is adequate time for give and take in the debate.

In addition, in my approach, the custodian would have these responsibilities:

to carefully examine the individual views of the problem and to determine how the individuals holding these views should be clustered into groups representing each of the major perspectives.

to manage the initial process of synthesis of the different views within each major perspective.

to manage and stimulate the commitment-building process once a final synthesis has been reached or a final decision on a strategic response has been selected in the absence of a final synthesis.

Without the use of structured conflict, the organization risks adopting either a solution based on only one perspective that ignores the critical aspects of the problem or a "patchwork" combination of solutions from different perspectives that do not fit together in any meaningful way. Through the use of structured devil's advocacy, it is more likely that solutions from multiple perspectives will be integrated into a coherent whole.

However, my approach has a number of advantages over traditional devil's advocacy. In organizations with multiple participants, each one may have a *somewhat* different view of the problem and its solution. If the more traditional approaches to devil's advocacy, multiple advocacy, or dialectical inquiry are used, the number of alternative views that must be discussed or debated could quickly become too large to be manageable. Some method is needed for reducing the alternatives to a reasonably small number that are *substantially* different from each other. Thus, I recommend that individual views consistent with each perspective be combined into one of the three major perspectives before the final discussion and consensus-building process. This will ensure that the views discussed will be manageable in number but will represent all the major perspectives for explaining and improving decisions.

Implications for Research

In the previous section of this chapter, I considered the implications of the three perspectives for the practice of strategic decision making. It is time now to turn to the implications for future research.

The recommendations for practice that I have just developed provide opportunities for research. I have suggested that my approach should be more effective than simple devil's advocacy, multiple advocacy, or dialectical inquiry. But this is an empirical question. Field and laboratory research of the type used to examine the effects of devil's advocacy and dialectical inquiry could be used to assess the effects of the approach I have recommended. However, the summaries of research within each perspective can also be used to identify research topics.

Within each of the three perspectives, there are many important questions that have not yet been answered. Many of these questions were identified in chapters 2, 3, and 4. However, in this chapter, I shall concentrate on research that deals with interfaces. Allison (1971, pp. 270–72) suggests that the use of models II and III in addition to model I analysis may improve our ability to predict decision outcomes. This is because these models sensitize us to different variables than those model I suggests are important. Model I suggests we attend to the beliefs and perceptions of key decision-makers and the sorts of rational goals that may be served by particular decisions. Model II directs us to organizational procedures and structural characteristics, while model III directs us to the political interests and political activities within the organization.

In chapter 5, I developed an integrative model of strategic decision making. However, this model was really only a brief outline of some of the ways cognitive, organizational, and political elements interact in strategic decisions. The model may help to identify questions for future research, but further empirical work is necessary to develop a truly integrative model.

Of course, past research has dealt with questions involving more than one perspective. Researchers have begun to explore these questions about connections between the perspectives. For example, some of the research on *organizational ideology*, as discussed in chapter 4, deals with the interface between cognitive and political processes. Some of this research focuses on the ways political processes may shape assumptions and the ways organizations may develop shared assumptions.

However, more research dealing with the interfaces between perspectives is needed in order to provide detail for the integrative model of strategic decisions. The following research questions deal with the interfaces between various perspectives. I do not intend that this should be an exhaustive list. Readers are encouraged to develop their own questions using this list as a stimulus.

The Cognitive/Organizational Interface

How do structural characteristics influence the effects of cognitive biases on strategic decisions? (Are the biases of key decisionmakers more likely to affect decision outcomes in highly centralized organizations?)

How does the level of formalization in the strategic decision-making process affect the assumptions and cognitive frames of key decisionmakers? (Do formalized decision processes produce more complex and accurate assumptions and cognitive frames?)

How does the complexity of key decisionmakers' cognitive frames affect the design of strategic planning systems? (Do decisionmakers with more complex cognitive frames opt for more comprehensive strategic planning systems?)

How does analogy to past problem situations affect the design of formal planning or decision-making processes?

How do strategic assumptions about important aspects of the company's environment and resources affect the design of strategic planning systems?

The Cognitive/Political Interface

How is the relative power of external influencers represented in decisionmakers' cognitive frames? (Do cognitive biases cause decisionmakers to over- or underestimate the power of particular influencers?)

How are resources such as information used in the process of political maneuvering to shape the cognitive frames of decisionmakers in order to promote and legitimate particular strategic alternatives? (How is information manipulated to encourage a particular strategic choice?)

How do the cognitive biases of organizational members affect their choice of tactics in political maneuvering? (Are particular tactics favored because of biased evaluations of their effectiveness?)

How do the strategic assumptions of key decisionmakers affect their identification of the most important external influencers?

The Organizational/Political Interface

How does the level of conflict between external influencers affect the characteristics of the organization's strategic decisionmaking processes? (Do organizations in highly conflictual environments have more complex and iterative decision processes?)

How does organizational structure affect the process of political maneuvering? (Are bargaining and maneuvering more intense in centralized or decentralized organizations?)

How does the number of important external influencers affect the structure of the organization (Are organizations with many external influencers more differentiated?)

The preceding list gives some of the research questions that can be identified using the model developed in chapter 5. Research on such topics will provide information on the complex relationships between cognitive, organizational, and political influences on decision outcomes.

Conclusion

In this book, I have described three basic approaches to explaining strategic decision outcomes and have summarized strategic management research consistent with each approach. I have also attempted to show how each approach to explaining decision outcomes leads to different sorts of prescriptions for improving future decisions.

Because of the complexity of strategic problems, it is unlikely that any single perspective will provide an adequate explanation for strategic decisions or an adequate set of prescriptions for improving future decisions. Therefore, it is necessary that multiple perspectives be combined. The principle of structured conflict, as embodied in various forms of devil's advocacy, provides one means for combining perspectives in practice. The development and refinement of an integrative model combining all three perspectives can be achieved through integrative research of the type just described. Such research may one day make it possible to provide a satisfactory answer to the question I posed in the first chapter, "Why do good companies develop bad strategies?" The answer to this question, in turn, may make it possible for good companies to develop better strategies in the future.

References

Abell, D., and Hammond, J. *Strategic Market Planning*. Englewood Cliffs, New Jersey: Prentice-Hall, 1979.

Abell, P. (ed.) *Organizations as Bargaining and Influence Systems*. New York: Halstead, 1975.

Allison, G.T. *The Essence of Decision*. Boston: Little, Brown, 1971.

Anderson, C., and Paine, F. Managerial perceptions and strategic behavior. *Academy of Management Journal*, 1975, *18*, 811–23.

Anderson, P.A. Decision-making by objection and the Cuban Missile Crisis. *Administrative Science Quarterly*, 1983, *28*, 201–22.

Andrews, K. *The Concept of Corporate Strategy*. Homewood, Illinois: Dow Jones-Irwin, 1971.

Ansoff, H. *Corporate Strategy*. New York: McGraw-Hill, 1965.

Armstrong, J.S. Advocacy and objectivity in science. *Management Science*, 1979, *23*, 423–28.

Astley, W.; Axelsson, R.; Butler, R.; Hickson, D.; and Wilson, D. Complexity and cleavage: Dual explanations of strategic decision making. *Journal of Management Studies*, 1982, *19*, 357–76.

Axelrod, R. *The Structure of Decision: Cognitive Maps of Political Elites*. Princeton, New Jersey: Princeton University Press, 1976.

Banks, R., and Wheelwright, S. Operations vs. strategy: Trading tomorrow for today. *Harvard Business Review*, 1979, *57*, 112–20.

Barley, S. Semiotics and the study of occupational and organizational cultures. *Administrative Science Quarterly*, 1983, *3*, 393–413.

Barnard, C.I. *The Functions of the Executive*. Cambridge, Massachusetts: Harvard University Press, 1938.

Barnes, J. Cognitive biases and their impact on strategic planning. *Strategic Management Journal*, 1984, *5*, 129–38.

Bateman, T., and Schwenk, C. Bias in investor decision-making. *Mid-American Journal of Business*, 1986, *1*, 5-11.

Blau, P. *Exchange and Power in Social Life*. New York: Wiley, 1964.

Bougon, M.G. Uncovering cognitive maps: The self-q technique. In G. Morgan (ed.), *Beyond Method*. Beverly Hills, California: Sage, 1983.

Bougon, M.; Weick, K.; and Binkhorst, B. Cognitions in organizations: An analysis of the Utrecht Jazz Orchestra. *Administrative Science Quarterly,* 1977, 22, 606–39.

Bourgeois, L. Performance and consensus. *Strategic Management Journal,* 1980, 1, 227–48.

Bourgeois, L. Strategic goals, perceived uncertainty, and economic performance in volatile environments. *Academy of Management Journal,* 1985, 28, 548–73.

Bracker, J. The historical development of the strategic management concept. *Academy of Management Review,* 1980, 5, 219-22.

Broms, H., and Gahmberg, H. Communication to self in organizations and cultures. *Administrative Science Quarterly,* 1983, 3, 482–95.

Brunsson, N. The irrationality of action and action rationality: Decisions, ideologies, and organizational actions. *Journal of Management Studies,* 1982, 19, 29–44.

Burgelman, R. A model of the interaction of strategic behavior, corporate extent, and the concept of strategy. *Academy of Management Review,* 1983(a), 8, 61–70.

Burgelman, R.A. A process model of internal corporate venturing in the diversified major firm. *Administrative Science Quarterly,* 1983(b), 28, 223–44.

Burgelman, R., and Sayles, L. *Inside Corporate Innovation.* New York: Free Press, 1986.

Business Week. Who's excellent now? November 5, 1984, 76–88.

Carroll, A., and Hoy, F. Integrating corporate social policy into strategic management. *Journal of Business Strategy,* 1984, 4, 48–57.

Chaffee, E. *Rational Decision-making in Higher Education.* Boulder, Colorado: National Center for Higher Education Management Systems, 1983.

Chaffee, E. Three models of strategy. *Academy of Management Review,* 1985, 10, 89–98.

Chandler, A. *Strategy and Structure.* Cambridge, Massachusetts: MIT Press, 1962.

Channon, D. Commentary on Grant and King's strategy formulation: Normative models. In D. Schendel and C. Hofer (eds.), *Strategic Management: A New View of Business Policy and Planning.* Boston: Little, Brown, 1979.

Chanin, M., and Shapiro, H. Dialectical inquiry in strategic planning. *Academy of Management Review.* 1985, 10, 663–75.

Chittipeddi, K., and Gioia, D. A cognitive psychological perspective on the strategic management process. Paper presented at the National Academy of Management meetings, 1983.

Christensen, C.; Andrews, K.; and Bower, J. *Business Policy.* Homewood, Illinois: Irwin, 1973.

Christensen, C.; Andrews, K.; Bower, J.; Hammermesh, K.; and Porter, M. *Business Policy.* Homewood, Illinois: Irwin, 1982.

Churchman, C.W. Hegelian inquiring systems. Internal working paper no. 49, Space Sciences Laboratory, Social Sciences Project, University of California, Berkeley, September 1966.

Cohen, M.D., and March, J.G. *Leadership and Ambiguity*. New York: McGraw-Hill, 1974.

Cohen, M.D.; March, J.G.; and Olsen, J.P. A garbage can model of organizational choice. *Administrative Science Quarterly*, 1972, *17*, 1–25.

Cosier, R.A. The effects of three potential aids for making strategic decision on prediction accuracy. *Organizational Behavior and Human Performance*, 1978, *22*, 295–306.

Cosier, R.A. Inquiry method, goal difficulty, and context effects on performance. *Decision Sciences*, 1980, *11*, 1–16.

Cosier, R.A. Dialectical inquiry in strategic planning: A case of premature acceptance? *Academy of Management Review*, 1981, 6, 643-48.

Cosier, R., and Rechner, P. Inquiry method effects on performance in a simulated business environment. *Organizational Behavior and Human Decision Processes*, 1985, *36*, 79–95.

Cosier, R.A.; Ruble, T.L.; and Alpin, J.C. An evaluation of the effectiveness of dialectical inquiry systems. *Management Science*, 1978, *24*, 1483–90.

Crozier, M. *The Bureaucratic Phenomenon*. Chicago: University of Chicago Press, 1964.

Cyert, R.M., and March, J.G. *A Behavioral Theory of the Firm*. Englewood Cliffs, New Jersey: Prentice-Hall, 1963.

Dandridge, T.; Mitroff, I.; and Joyce, A. Organizational symbolism: A topic to expand organizational analysis. *Academy of Management Review*, 1980, *5*, 77–82.

Deal, T.A., and Kennedy, A.A. *Corporate Culture*. Reading, Massachusetts: Addison-Wesley, 1982.

de Rivera, J. *The Psychological Dimension of Foreign Policy*. Columbus, Ohio: Charles E. Merrill, 1968.

De Woot, P.; Heyvaert, H.; and Martou, F. Strategic management. *International Studies of Management and Organization*, 1977, *7*, 60–75.

Diffenbach, J. Influence diagrams for complex strategic issues. *Strategic Management Journal*, 1982, *3*, 133–46.

Dirsmith, M., and Covaleski, M. Strategy, external communication and environmental context. *Strategic Management Journal*, 1983, *4*, 137–51.

Dirsmith, M.; Jablonski, S.; and Luzi, A. Planning and control in the U.S. federal government. *Strategic Management Journal*, 1980, *1*, 303–30.

Downs, A. *Inside Bureaucracy*. Boston: Little, Brown, 1967.

Duhaime, I.D., and Schwenk, C. Conjectures on cognitive simplication in acquisition and divestment decision-making. *Academy of Management Review*, 1985, *10*, 287–95.

Dunbar, R.M.; Dutton, J.; and Torbert, W. Crossing mother: Ideological constraints on organizational improvements. *Journal of Management Studies*, 1982, *19*, 91–108.

Dutton, J.; Fahey, L.; and Narayanan, V. Toward understanding strategic issue diagnosis. *Strategic Management Journal*, 1983, *4*, 307–23.

Eden, C.; Jones, S.; and Sims, D. *Thinking in Organizations*. London: Macmillan, 1979.

Eden, C.; Jones, S.; and Sims, D. *Messing About in Problems*. Oxford, England: Pergamon, 1983.

Emerson, R. Power-Dependence Relations. *American Sociological Review*, 1962, 27, 31–41.

Emshoff, J.R., and Finnel, A. Defining corporate strategy: A case study using strategic assumptions analysis. Working paper no. 8-78, Wharton Applied Research Center, Philadelphia, October 1978.

Epstein, E., *The Corporation in American Politics*. Englewood Cliffs, New Jersey: Prentice-Hall, 1969.

Etzioni, A. Mixed scanning: A third approach to decision making. *Public Administration Review*, 1967, 27, 385–92.

Fahey, L. On strategic management decision processes. *Strategic Management Journal*, 1981, 2, 43–60.

Fahey, L., and King, W. Environmental scanning for strategic planning. *Business Horizons*. August 1977, 61–71.

Farrell, D., and Petersen, J. Patterns of political behavior in organizations. *Academy of Management Review*, 1982, 7, 403–12.

Feldman, J. Beyond attribution theory: Cognitive processes in performance appraisal. *Journal of Applied Psychology*, 1981, 66, 127–48.

Feldman, M.S., and March, J.G. Information in organizations as signal and symbol. *Administrative Science Quarterly*, 1981, 26, 171–86.

Fiol, M., and Lyles, M. Organizational learning. *Academy of Management Review*, 1985, 10, 803–13.

Ford, J. Effects of causal attributions on decision-makers' responses to performance downturns. *Academy of Management Review*, 1985, 10, 770–86.

Ford, J., and Hegarty, H. Decision makers' beliefs about hte causes and effects of structure. *Academy of Management Journal*, 1984, 27, 271–91.

Fredrickson, J. The comprehensiveness of strategic decision processes. *Academy of Management Journal*, 1984, 27, 445–66.

Fredrickson, J. The strategic decision process and organizational structure. *Academy of Management Review*, 1986, 11, 280–97.

Fredrickson, J., and Mitchell, T. Strategic decision processes. *Academy of Management Journal*, 1984, 27, 399–423.

Freeman, R. *Strategic Management: A Stakeholder Approach*. Boston: Pitman, 1984.

French, J.P., and Raven, B. The bases of social power. In D.Cartwright (ed.), *Studies in Social Power*. Ann Arbor, Michigan: Institute for Social Research, 1959.

Galbraith, J., and Kazanjian, R. *Strategy Implementation: Structure, Systems, and Process*. St. Paul, Minnesota: West, 1986.

George, A. The case for multiple advocacy in making foreign policy. *American Political Science Review*, 1972, 66, 751–85.

George, A. *Presidential Decision Making*. Boulder, Colorado: Westview, 1980.

Gilovich, T. Seeing the past in the present: The effect of associations to familiar events on judgments and decisions. *Journal of Personality and Social Psychology,* 1981, *40,* 797–808.

Gioia, D., and Poole, P. Scripts in organizational behavior. *Academy of Management Review,* 1984, *9,* 449–59.

Gordon, W. *Synectics.* New York: Harper & Row, 1961.

Grant, J., and King, W. *The Logic of Strategic Planning.* St. Paul, Minnesota: West, 1982.

Grinyer, P., and Norburn, D. Planning for existing markets. *International Studies of Management and Organization,* 1977, *7,* 99–122.

Gupta, A. Contingency linkages. *Academy of Management Review,* 1984, *1,* 399–412.

Gupta, A., and Govindarajan, V. Business unit strategy, managerial characteristics, and business unit effectiveness. *Academy of Management Journal,* 1984, *27,* 25–41.

Hall, D., and Saias, M. Strategy follows structure. *Strategic Management Journal,* 1980, *1,* 149–64.

Hall, P. *Great Planning Disasters.* Berkeley: University of California Press, 1982.

Hambrick, D. Environment, strategy, and power within top management teams. *Administrative Science Quarterly,* 1981, *26,* 253–76.

Hambrick, D. High profit strategies in mature capital goods industries. *Academy of Management Journal,* 1983, *26,* 687–707.

Hambrick D., and Lei, D. Toward an empirical prioritization of contingency variables for business strategy. *Academy of Management Journal,* 1985, *28,* 763–88.

Hambrick, D., and Mason, P. Upper echelons: The organization as a reflection of its top managers. *Academy of Management Review,* 1984, *9,* 193–206.

Hanus, B. QUEST: A quick environmental scanning technique. *Long Range Planning,* 1982, *15,* 39–45.

Harrigan, K. *Strategies for Declining Businesses.* Lexington, Massachusetts: Lexington Books, 1980.

Harrigan, K. *Strategies for Vertical Integration.* Lexington, Massachusetts: Lexington Books, 1983.

Harrigan, K. *Strategies for Joint Ventures.* Lexington, Massachusetts: Lexington Books, 1985.

Hatten, K.; Schendel, D.; and Cooper, A. A strategic model for the U.S. brewing industry. *Academy of Management Journal,* 1978, *21,* 592–610.

Hedberg, B. How organizations learn and unlearn. In P. Nystrom and W. Starbuck (eds.) *Handbook of Organizational Design.* London: Oxford University Press, 1981.

Henderson, B. *Henderson on Corporate Strategy.* Cambridge, Massachusetts: Abt Books, 1979.

Herbert, T.T., and Estes, R.W. Improving executive planning by formalizing dissent: The corporate devil's advocate. *Academy of Management Review,* 1977, *2,* 662–67.

Hickson, D.; Hinings, C.; Lee, C.; Schneck, R.; and Pennings, J. A strategic contingencies theory of intraorganizational power. *Administrative Science Quarterly,* 1971, *16,* 216–29.

Hirschman, A. *Exit, Voice, and Loyalty.* Cambridge, England: Cambridge University Press, 1970.

Hofer, C., and Haller, T. GLOBESCAN: A way to better international risk assessment. *Journal of Business Strategy,* 1980, *1,* 41–55.

Hofer, C.W., and Schendel, D. *Strategy Formulation: Analytical Concepts.* St. Paul, Minnesota: West, 1978.

Hogarth, R.M. *Judgment and Choice: The Psychology of Decision.* Chichester, England: Wiley, 1980.

Hogarth, R.M., and Makridakis, S. Forecasting and planning: An evaluation. *Management Science,* 1981, *27,* 115–38.

Huff, A. Evocative metaphors. *Human Systems Management,* 1980, *1,* 1–10.

Huff, A. Industry influences on strategy reformulation. *Strategic Management Journal,* 1982, *3,* 119–31.

Huff, A., and Schwenk, C. Bias and sensemaking in good times and bad. Working paper, University of Illinois, at Champaign-Urbana 1986.

Isenberg, D. How senior managers think (and what about). Unpublished manuscript, Harvard University, Cambridge, Massachusetts, 1983.

Janis, I.L. *Victims of GroupThink.* Boston: Houghton Mifflin, 1972.

Janis, I.L., and Mann, L. *Decision Making: A Psychological Analysis of Conflict, Choice, and Commitment.* New York: Free Press, 1977.

Jemison, D. Organizational versus environmental sources of influence in strategic decision making. *Strategic Management Journal,* 1981(a), *2,* 77–89.

Jemison, D. The importance of an integrative approach to strategic management. *Academy of Management Review,* 1981(b), *6,* 601–8.

Jemison, D. The importance of boundary spanning roles in strategic decision-making. *Journal of Management Studies,* 1984, *2,* 131–52.

Jervis, R. Hypothesis on misperceptions. *World Politics,* April 1968, *20,* 457–74.

Jervis, R. *Perception and Misperception in International Politics.* Princeton, New Jersey: Princeton University Press, 1976.

Jick, T.D. Mixing qualitative and quantitative methods: Triangulation in action. *Administrative Science Quarterly,* 1979, *24,* 602–11.

Johnson, D., and Tjosvold, D. Constructive controversy. In D. Tjosvold and D. Johnson (eds.), *Conflicts in Organizations.* New York: Irvington, 1983.

Kanter, R.M. *Men and Women of the Corporation.* New York: Basic Books, 1977.

Kennedy, R.F. *Thirteen Days.* New York: Norton, 1969.

Kessel, J. Government structure and political environment: A statistical note about American cities. *American Political Science Review,* 1962, *56,* 615–20.

Kets de Vries, M., and Miller, D. *The Neurotic Organization.* San Francisco: Jossey-Bass, 1984.

Kinder, D.R., and Weiss, J.A. In lieu of rationality: Psychological perspectives on foreign policy decision-making. *Journal of Conflict Resolution,* 1978, *22,* 707–35.

Klein, H., and Linneman, R. The use of scenarios in corporate planning—Eight case histories. *Long Range Planning*, 1981, *14*, 69–77.

Klein, H., and Newman, W. How to use SPIRE. *Journal of Business Strategy*, 1980, *1*, 32–45.

Lang, J.R.; Dittrich, J.E.; and White, S.E. Managerial problem-solving methods: A review and a proposal. *Academy of Management Review*, 1978, *3*, 854–65.

Langer, E.J. *The Psychology of Control.* Beverly Hills, California: Sage, 1983.

Larreche, J., and Srinivasan, V. STRATPORT: A decision support system for strategic planning. *Journal of Marketing*, 1981, *45*, 39–52.

Lawrence, P., and Lorsch, J. *Organization and Environment.* Homewood, Illinois: Irwin, 1969.

Levin, H. *Grand Delusions.* New York: Viking, 1983.

Lind, E., and Walker, L. Theory testing, theory development and laboratory research on legal issues. *Law and Human Behavior*, 1979, *3*, 5–19.

Lindblom, C.E. The science of "muddling through." *Public Administration Review*, Spring 1959, 79–88.

Linneman, R., and Klein, H. The use of multiple scenarios by U.S. industrial companies. *Long Range Planning*, 1983, *16*, 94–101.

Linstone, H.A., and Turoff, M. *The Delphi Methods: Techniques and Applications.* Reading, Massachusetts: Addison-Wesley, 1975.

Lorange, P., and Vancil, R. *Strategic Planning Systems.* Englewood Cliffs, New Jersey: Prentice-Hall, 1977.

Louis, M.R. A cultural perspective on organizations. Paper presented at the National Academy of Management meetings, 1980.

Lyles, M. Formulating strategic problems: Empirical analysis and model development. *Strategic Management Journal*, 1981, *2*, 61–75.

Lyles, M., and Mitroff, I.I. Organization problem formulation: An empirical study. *Administrative Science Quarterly*, 1980, *25*, 109–19.

Lyles, M., and Schwenk, C. The development and maintenance of organizational schemata. Unpublished working paper, University of Illinois at Champaign-Urbana. 1986.

MacMillan, I. *Strategy Formulation: Political Concepts.* St. Paul, Minnesota: West, 1978.

MacMillan, I., and Jones, P. *Strategy Formulation: Power and Politics.* St. Paul, Minnesota: West, 1986.

March, J.G., and Olsen, J.P. *Ambiguity and Choice in Organizations.* Bergen, Norway: Universitestsforlaget, 1979.

March, J.G., and Simon, H. A. *Organizations.* New York: Wiley, 1958.

Martin, J.; Feldman, M; Hatch, M.; and Sitkin, S. The uniqueness paradox in organizational stories. *Administrative Science Quarterly*, 1983, *3*, 438–53.

Mason, R. A dialectical approach to strategic planning. *Management Science*, 1969, *15*, B403–14.

Mason, R.O., and Mitroff, I.I. *Challenging Strategic Planning Assumptions.* New York: Wiley, 1981.

May, E. *"Lessons" of the Past.* New York: Oxford University Press, 1973.

Mazzolini, R. *Government Controlled Enterprises.* New York: Wiley, 1979.

Mazzolini, R. How strategic decisions are made. *Long Range Planning.* 1981, *14*, 85–96.

McCaskey, M. *The Executive Challenge.* Marshfield, Massachusetts: Pitman, 1982.

McNamee, P. *Tools and Techniques for Strategic Management.* London: Pergamon, 1985.

Meyer, A. How ideologies supplant formal structures and shape responses to environments. *Journal of Management Studies,* 1982, *19*, 45–62.

Meyer, A. Mingling decision-making metaphors. *Academy of Management Review,* 1984, *9*, 6–17.

Miles, R. *Coffin Nails and Corporate Strategies.* Englewood Cliffs, New Jersey: Prentice-Hall, 1982.

Miles, R., and Snow, C. *Organizational Strategy, Structure, and Process.* New York: McGraw-Hill, 1978.

Miller, D., and Friesen, P. Momentum and revolution in organizational adaptation. *Academy of Management Journal,* 1980, *23*, 591–614.

Miller, D. and Friesen, P. Structural change and performance: Quantum versus piecemeal-incremental approaches. *Academy of Management Journal,* 1982, *4*, 867–92.

Miller, D., and Friesen, P. Strategy making and the environment. *Strategic Management Journal,* 1983, *4*, 221–35.

Miller, D.; Kets de Vries, M.; and Toulouse, J. Top executive locus of control and its relationship to strategy-making, structure, and environment. *Academy of Management Journal,* 1982, *25*, 237–53.

Mintzberg, H. Strategy making in three modes. *California Management Review,* Winter 1973, 44–53.

Mintzberg, H. Patterns in strategy formulation. *Management Science,* 1978, *24*, 934–48.

Mintzberg, H. *Power In and Around Organizations.* Englewood Cliffs, New Jersey: Prentice-Hall, 1983.

Mintzberg, H. Power and organizational life cycles. *Academy of Management Review,* 1984, *9*, 207–24.

Mintzberg, H., and Waters, J. Tracking strategy in the entrepreneurial firm. *Academy of Management Journal,* 1982, *25*, 465–99.

Mintzberg, H.; Raisinghani, P.; and Theoret, A. The structure of "unstructured" decision processes. *Administrative Science Quarterly,* 1976, *2*, 246–75.

Mitroff, I.I. The myth of objectivity or why science needs a new psychology of science. *Management Science,* 1972, *18*, B613–18.

Mitroff, I.I.; Barabba, V.P.; and Kilmann, R.H. The application of behavioral and philosophical technologies to strategic planning: A case study of a large federal agency. *Management Science,* 1977, *23*, 44–58.

Mitroff, I.I.; Emshoff, J.R.; and Kilmann, R.H. Assumptional analysis: A methodology for strategic problem-solving. *Management Science,* 1979, *25*, 583–93.

Mitroff, I.I., and Mason, R. The metaphysics of policy and planning: A reply to Cosier. *Academy of Management Review*, 1981, *6*, 649–652.

Mitroff, I., and Mason, R. Business policy and metaphysics: Some philosophical considerations. *Academy of Management Review*, 1982, *7*, 361–70.

Murray, E. Strategic choice as a negotiated outcome. *Management Science*, 1978, *24*, 960–72.

Narayanan, V., and Fahey, L. The micro-politics of strategy formulation. *Academy of Management Review*, 1982, *7*, 25–34.

Naylor, T. *Corporate Planning Models.* Reading, Massachusetts: Addison-Wesley, 1979.

Neisser, U. *Cognition and Reality.* San Francisco: W.H. Freeman, 1976.

Neustadt, R. *Presidential Power: The Politics of Leadership.* New York: Mentor, 1960.

Nielson, R. Towards a method for building consensus during strategic planning. *Sloan Management Review*, 1981. *23*, 29–40.

Nisbett, R., and Ross, L. *Human Inference.* Englewood Cliffs, New Jersey: Prentice-Hall, 1980.

Nutt, P.C. Planning process archetypes and their effectiveness. *Decision Sciences*, 1984(a), *15*, 221–38.

Nutt, P. Types of organizational decision processes. *Administrative Science Quarterly*, 1984(b), *29*, 414–50.

Parsons, T. *Structure and Process in Modern Societies.* Glencoe, Illinois: Free Press, 1960.

Peters, T.J., and Waterman, R.H. *In Search of Excellence.* New York: Harper & Row, 1982.

Pettigrew, A. On studying organizational culture. *Administrative Science Quarterly, 1979, 24*, 570–81.

Pfeffer, J. *Power in Organizations.* Marshfield, Massachusetts: Pitman, 1981.

Pfeffer, J., and Salancik, J. *The External Control of Organizations.* New York: Harper & Row, 1978.

Pickle, H., and Friedlander, F. Seven societal criteria of organizational success. *Personnel Psychology, 1967, 20*, 165–78.

Pondy, L. The role of metaphors and myths in organization and in the facilitation of change. In L. Pondy, P. Frost, G. Morgan, and T. Dandridge (eds.), *Organizational Symbolism.* Greenwich, Connecticut: JAI Press, 1983.

Pondy, L., and Huff, A. Budget cutting in Riverside: Emergent policy reframing as a process of conflict minimization. Unpublished manuscript, University of Illinois at Champaign-Urbana, 1983.

Porter, M. *Competitive Strategy.* New York: Free Press, 1980.

Pounds, W.F. The process of problem finding. *Industrial Management Review*, 1969, *11*, 1–19.

Preble, J.F. Future forecasting with LEAP. *Long Range Planning*, 1982, *15*, 64–69.

Quinn, J.B. *Strategies for Change: Logical Incrementalism.* Homewood, Illinois: Irvin, 1980.

Reedy, G. *The Twilight of the Presidency.* New York: World, 1970.

Rhenman, E. *Organization Theory for Long-Range Planning.* New York: Wiley, 1973.

Rhodes S., and Schwenk, C. Devil's advocates in presidential decision-making. Paper presented at the annual Midwest Political Science Association meetings, Chicago, 1983.

Riley, P. A structuralist account of political cultures. *Administrative Science Quarterly, 1983, 3,* 414–37.

Robey, D., and Taggart, W. Measuring managers' minds. *Academy of Management Review,* 1981, *6,* 375–84.

Robinson, R. The importance of "outsiders" in small firm strategic planning. *Academy of Management Journal,* 1982, *25,* 90–93.

Ross, S. Complexity and the presidency. In R. Axelrod (ed.), *The Structure of Decision: Cognitive Maps of Political Elites.* Princeton, New Jersey: Princeton University Press, 1976.

Rourke, F.E. *Bureaucratic Power in National Politics.* Boston: Little, Brown, 1965.

Rumelhart, D., and Ortony, A. The representation of knowledge in memory. In R. Anderson, R. Spiro, and W. Montague (eds.), *Schooling and the Acquisition of Knowledge.* Hillsdale, New Jersey: Lawrence Erlbaum, 1977.

Sapienza, A.M. A cognitive perspective on strategy formulation. Paper presented at the Academy of Management national meetings, Dallas, August 1983.

Schall, M. A communication-rules approach to organizational culture. *Administrative Science Quarterly,* 1983, *28,* 542–56.

Schendel, D., and Hofer, C. *Strategic Management.* Boston: Little, Brown, 1979.

Schlaim, A. Failures in national intelligence estimates: The case of the Yom Kippur War. *World Politics,* April 1976, 355–78.

Schoeffler, S. Cross-sectional study of strategy, structure, and performance aspects of the PIMS program. In H. Thorelli (ed.), *Strategy + Structure = Performance.* Bloomington, Indiana: Indiana University Press, 1977.

Schon, D. Generative metaphor: A perspective on problem-setting in social policy. In A. Ortony (ed.), *Metaphor and Thought.* New York: Cambridge University Press, 1979.

Schrader, C.; Taylor. L.; and Dalton, D. Strategic planning and organizational performance. *Journal of Management,* 1984. *10,* 149–71.

Schwartz, H., and David, S. Matching corporate culture and business strategy. *Organizational Dynamics,* 1981, *10,* 30–48.

Schweiger, D., and Finger, P. The comparative effectiveness of dialectical inquiry and devil's advocacy: The impact of task biases and previous research findings. *Strategic Management Journal,* 1984, *5,* 335–50.

Schweiger, D.; Sandberg, W.; and Ragan, J. Group approaches for improving strategic decision making: A comparative analysis of dialectical inquiry, devil's advocacy, and consensus. *Academy of Management Journal,* 1986, *29,* 51–71.

Schwenk, C.R. Effects of inquiry methods nad ambiguity tolerance on prediction performance. *Decision Sciences,* 1982, *13,* 207–21.

Schwenk C. Inquiry method effects on prediction performance: Task involvement as a mediating variable. *Decision Sciences,* 1984(a), *15,* 449–62.

Schwenk, C.R. Effects of planning aids and presentation media on performance and affective responses in strategic decision-making. *Management Science,* 1984(b), *30,* 263–72.

Schwenk, C. Devil's advocacy in managerial decision-making. *Journal of Management Studies,* 1984(c), *21,* 153–68.

Schwenk, C. Cognitive simplification processes in strategic decision-making. *Strategic Management Journal,* 1984(d), *5,* 111–28.

Schwenk, C. Giving the devil its due. *The Wharton Annual,* 1985(a), 104–8.

Schwenk, C. The use of participant recollection in the modeling of organizational decision processes. *Academy of Management Review,* 1985(b), *10,* 496–503.

Schwenk, C. The essence of strategic decision. Working paper, University of Illinois at Champaign-Urbana, 1985(c).

Schwenk, C. Information, cognitive bias, and commitment to a course of action. *Academy of Management Review,* 1986, *11,* 298–310.

Schwenk, C.R., and Cosier, R. Effects of the expert, devil's advocate, and dialectical inquiry methods on prediction performance. *Organizational Behavior and Human Performance,* 1980, *26,* 409–23.

Schwenk, C., and Huff, A. Argumentation in strategic decision-making. In D. Lamb and P. Shrivastava (eds.), *Advances in Strategic Management.* Greenwich, Connecticut: JAI Press, 1986, 189–202.

Schwenk, C.R., and Thomas, H. Effects on conflicting analyses on managerial decision-making. *Decision Sciences,* 1983(a), *14,* 467–82.

Schwenk, C.R., and Thomas, H. Formulating the mess: The role of decision aids in problem formulation. *Omega,* 1983(b), *11,* 239–52.

Selznick, P. *TVA and the Grass Roots.* Berkeley: University of California Press, 1949.

Selznick, P. *Leadership and Administration.* Evanston, Illinois: Row, Peterson, 1957.

Sergiovanni, T., and Corbally, J. *Leadership and Organizational Culture.* Urbana, Illinois: University of Illinois Press, 1984.

Sexty, R. Autonomy strategies of government owned business corporations in Canada. *Strategic Management Journal,* 1980, *1,* 371–84.

Shrader, C.; Taylor, L.; and Dalton, D. Strategic planning and organizational performance: A critical appraisal. *Journal of Management,* 1984, *10,* 149–71.

Shrivastava, P. A typology of organizational learning systems. *Journal of Management Studies,* 1983, *20,* 7–28.

Shrivastava, P., and Dutton, J. Studying assumptions underlying policy makers' thinking. Paper presented at the Academy of Management national meetings, Dallas, August 1983.

Shrivastava, P., and Lim, G. Alternative approaches to strategic analysis of environments. Working paper, New York University, New York, 1984.

Shrivastava, P., and Mitroff, I. Frames of reference managers use: A study in applied sociology of knowledge. In R. Lamb (ed.), *Advances in Strategic Management*. Greenwich, Connecticut: JAI Press, 1983.

Shrivastava, P., and Mitroff, I. Enhancing organizational research utilization: The role of decision makers' assumptions. *Academy of Management Review*, 1984, *9*, 18–26.

Simon, H.A. *Models of Man*. New York: Wiley, 1957.

Simon, H.A. *Administrative Behavior* (third edition). New York: Free Press, 1976.

Slovic, P.; Fischhoff, B.; and Lichtenstein, S. Behavioral decision theory. *Annual Review of Psychology*, 1977, *28*, 1–39.

Spekman, R. Influence and information: An explanatory investigation of the boundary role person's basis of power. *Academy of Management Journal*, 1979, *1*, 104–17.

Starbuck, W. Congealing oil: Inventing ideologies to justify acting ideologies out. *Journal of Management Studies*, 1982, *19*, 3–28.

Steinbruner, J.D. *The Cybernetic Theory of Decision*. Princeton, New Jersey: Princeton University Press, 1974.

Steiner, G.A. *Strategic Planning: What Every Manager Must Know*. New York: Free Press, 1979.

Stubbart, C., and Ramaprasad, A. An interpretive examination of a strategic decision-maker's beliefs about the steel industry. Paper presented at the Academy of Management meetings, San Diego, 1985.

Summer, C.E. *Strategic Behavior in Business and Government*. Boston: Little, Brown, 1980.

Taggart, W., and Robey, D. Minds and managers. *Academy of Management Review*, 1981, *6*, 187–96.

Taylor, R.N. Psychological determinants of bounded rationality: Implications for decision-making. *Decision Sciences*, 1975, *6*, 409–29.

Taylor, S. The interface of cognitive and social psychology. In J. Harvey (ed.), *Cognition, Social Behavior and the Environment*. Hillsdale, New Jersey: Lawrence Erlbaum, 1982.

Taylor, S., and Crocker, J. Schematic bases of social information processing. In E. Higgens, C. Herman, and J. Zauna, (eds.), *Social Cognition: The Ontario Symposium*. Hillsdale, New Jersey: Lawrence Erlbaum, 1983.

Thomas, H. and Schwenk, C. Problem formulation and the consultant-client relationship. *Interfaces*, 1983, *13*, 25–39.

Thompson, J.C. How could Vietnam happen? An autopsy. *Atlantic Monthly*, April 1968, 47–53.

Thompson, J.D. *Organizations in Action*. New York: McGraw-Hill, 1967.

Tilles, S. How to evaluate corporate strategy. *Harvard Business Review*, 1963, *41*, 111–21.

Tjosvold, D. Effects of approach to controversy on superiors' incorporation of subordinates' information in decision-making. *Journal of Applied Psychology*, 1982, *67*, 189–93.

Tjosvold, D. Implications of controversy research for management. *Journal of Management*, 1985, *11*, 21–37.

Tolman. E. Cognitive maps in rats and men. *Psychological Review,* 1948, *55,* 189–208.

Tsujimoto, R.; Wilde, J.; and Robertson, D. Distorted memory for exemplars of a social structure: Evidence for schematic memory processes. *Journal of Personality and Social Psychology,* 1978, *36,* 1402–14.

Tversky, A., and Kahneman, D. Judgment under uncertainty: Heuristics and biases. *Science,* 1974, *185,* 1124–31.

Ungson, G.; Braunstein, D.; and Hall, P. Managerial information processing: A research review. *Administrative Science Quarterly,* 1981, *26,* 116–34.

Van Gundy, A. *Techniques for Structured Problem-Solving.* New York: Van Nostrand Reinhold, 1981.

Weick, K. Cognitive processes in organizations. In B. Staw, (ed.), *Research in Organizational Behavior.* Greenwich, Connecticut: JAI Press, 1979.

Williamson, O. *Markets and Hierarchies.* New York: Free Press, 1975.

Wilson, I. Reforming the strategic planning processes: Integration of social and business needs. *Long Range Planning,* October 1974, 2–6.

Witte, E. Field research on complex decision-making processes—the phase theorem. *International Studies of Management and Organization,* 1972, 156–82.

Woo, C. Market share leadership—not always so good. *Harvard Business Review,* January-February 1984.

Zeithmal, C.; Kleim, G.; and Baysinger, B. Toward an integrated strategic management process: An empirical review of corporate political strategy. Unpublished manuscript, Texas A & M University, College Station, 1982.

Index

About the Author

Charles Schwenk received his MBA and DBA degrees from Indiana University and taught from 1980 to 1986 at the University of Illinois in Champaign-Urbana. He is now an associate professor of management at Indiana University.

Professor Schwenk has published articles on strategic decision making in *Academy of Management Review, Decision Sciences, Journal of Management Studies, Management Science, Organizational Behavior and Human Decision Processes,* and *Strategic Management Journal.* He currently serves on the editorial review boards of *Academy of Management Review* and *Strategic Management Journal.*